Contents

To my mother
Beulah Harris Cauthen
and
To my daughters
Nancy Kathleen Cauthen
Melissa Anne Cauthen

Love gave me life.
Life gave me love.
Having received,
I want to give
A love of life,
A life of love.
The torch of life,
The flame of love.
Generations pass,
The glow goes on.

THE ETHICS OF ENJOYMENT

The Christian's Pursuit of Happiness

by

Kenneth Cauthen

JOHN KNOX PRESS
ATLANTA

Library of Congress Cataloging in Publication Data
Cauthen, Wilfred Kenneth.
The ethics of enjoyment.

Includes bibliographical references.
1. Social history—1960- 2. Social ethics.
3. Church and social problems. 4. Technology and ethics. I. Title.
HN18.C32 261.8 75-13466
ISBN 0-8042-0815-8

Printed in the United States of America

CHAPTER 1

Is There Any Hope?

A vague uneasiness is abroad in the land. It is shared to some degree by nearly everyone who reads the newspapers and watches the evening news on TV. In the film *The Graduate*, Benjamin is asked why he is so glum at the party arranged by his parents to celebrate his graduation from college. "I'm just a little worried about my future," he says. Most of us are these days. We are anxious about what is happening in our country. We are concerned about where the human race is going. We wonder what will happen to us and our children. Thousands are dying of starvation in Asia and Africa. Inflation and recession deal a double blow at home. Prices rise and unemployment increases. In order to feed, clothe, and house a growing world population, economic growth must speed up. But increasing production pollutes the air, the land, and the sea. It also runs the risk of using up certain nonrenewable natural resources. In particular, energy sources are limited. Even if an inexhaustible supply of energy were available, danger still lies ahead. The production of goods requires energy. Energy throws waste heat into the environment. There are limits to the amount of heat that the earth can absorb without warming up so much that it becomes uninhabitable.

The industrial world tells the poor countries to reduce their birthrates, since overpopulation is so dangerous. They reply that the rich nations must reduce their extravagant consumption and share their bounty with the rest of the world. In the second round of discussion, the affluent nations claim that, after all, they produced most of this wealth, so they have a right to enjoy it. The underdeveloped countries come back by saying,

"Yes, you have produced enormous wealth. But you did it partly by exploiting us and using up our natural resources." The average citizen everywhere hardly knows what to think. A distinguished biologist looking at the situation concludes that it will be impossible to feed everybody right away, no matter what we do. Imagine the *Titanic* sinking in the distance. The lifeboat will hold only 50. There are 150 people floundering in the ocean crying for help. Against that background, Garrett Hardin makes this case *against* helping the poor: to attempt to feed all now only means that more than ever will be born to starve later.[1]

Local wars keep popping up. The Middle East remains a powder keg. Even now Russia and the United States have missiles aimed at each other's cities. The prospect is that more nations will soon be able to make nuclear weapons. Looking at this situation, a leading economist suggests that countries with an increasing scarcity of food may well fall into the hands of strong-arm dictators. Authoritarian government may be inevitable where mass starvation generates social chaos. And once these tyrants are armed with nuclear weapons, the industrial nations may confront blackmail. A massive transfer of wealth to the poor may be demanded as the price of saving some large city from nuclear holocaust.[2]

If these global terrors are not enough, there is the recent suggestion that the lowly aerosol can will do us in. The spray that holds our hair in place and keeps our underarms dry releases chemicals that rise up toward the heavens. There they destroy the layer of ozone that screens out some of the sun's destructive rays. Should one laugh or cry at this prospect? Probably the first thing we should do is keep our common sense and recall that most predictions of doomsday turn out to be nonsense. Indeed, pronouncements about the future are famous for their inaccuracy. The well-known surgeon, Alfred Velpeau, wrote in 1839 that pain would always be associated with surgery. It was absurd, he said, to think otherwise. A week before the first flight of the Wright brothers at Kitty Hawk, the *New York Times* urged a rival plane-builder to give up such wasteful experiments. The editorial urged Professor Langley to use his scientific talents for better purposes than trying to fly. Surely there must have been someone who came up with a projection of trends about 1890 that showed conclusively that by 1975 the streets of New York City would be six feet deep in horse manure. Not long ago, Kenneth Boulding was asked about the alleged "aerosol-can ozone crisis." He replied that science was in danger of losing its credibility with the public as the result of such scares. He reminded the audience that most of them are based on very scanty evidence.

Nevertheless, many problems are real enough. Even when we allow for hysteria and exaggeration, it remains true that enormous challenges lie ahead for the human race. We may pretend they do not exist. But we cannot wish them away. Our discomfort has two sides to it. One aspect is that there is good reason to be anxious about the future, since the problems are so difficult. The other part of it is that we have doubts about our ability to cope with these dangers. The primary issue here is not simply whether "the human race" as a whole can guide itself through the perils of the next few years safely and perhaps even realize the promises of the future—indeed, the promises are as astounding as the threats. The more immediate concern is the bafflement that individuals feel, which I feel, in confronting these huge global issues. Do you recognize your own thoughts in the following statement?

> I would like to be a good world-citizen and make life better for myself and others. My problem is that the world has become so complicated that I no longer know what I should do. Can I do anything that really makes a difference? Sure, I can give money to good causes and help needy individuals and families as opportunities arise. But the big problems that affect what life is going to be like for most people in the near future are overwhelming. We seem caught up in forces beyond our power to control. Yet these forces will determine whether millions of people have food and shelter and jobs and a chance for some kind of decent existence. I mean problems like the nuclear arms race, inflation, the population explosion, pollution,

world hunger, the energy shortage, health care, welfare, and so on. How can you connect an individual's actions with problems as big as that? Isn't the world too complicated to understand or to do anything about?

If you are one of the millions of Americans who are "a little worried about the future" and wonder what it means to be responsible to others in today's world, then this book may be for you. It is intended to speak to people who really want to live out their religious faith in ways that make a real difference for themselves and others. It is directed to those who feel overwhelmed by the complexity of the issues they face. Granted that we ought to love our neighbors and seek justice for all, what does that mean in the complicated world of today? Is there any hope? What are our chances for peace and happiness in the years ahead? Can we leave our children a decent world and the prospect of a future in which they can find their own joy and peace? These are the questions I intend to deal with.

Two features of our complicated world stand out at once. Both are crucial to the problem of living out our faith in everyday life.

1. The first is that the work of the world is increasingly carried on in large organizations in which the individual seems swallowed up. Hospitals, schools, corporations, charities, labor unions, agribusinesses (huge farming corporations), and others that we could name all form a complex web. These organizations grow our food, manufacture necessary goods, and build our houses. They also provide health care, education, transportation, communication, and other services that make life possible in our society. The largest organization of all is government—the overseer and policymaker whose responsibility it is to give some order and direction to our common life. The way these systems work separately and interact determines to a large measure whether there are jobs for everybody at decent wages, whether everybody has enough food, a comfortable place to live, and the opportunities to make the best of his or her talents.

If visions of the good life are to have any effect on the actual quality of life, they must find their way into this system of organizations. Rescuing the perishing today is not primarily a matter of lending a helping hand to individuals injured or robbed on the road to Jericho. Rather it means creating a safe and efficient transportation system. It means providing hospitals and doctors that the poor as well as the affluent can afford. However, recognizing that we need a strategy in dealing with organizations just as we need principles in dealing with individuals is only part of the complexity of being morally responsible today.

2. We have increasingly become aware that to the whole set of problems that go under the heading of peace and social justice we must now add another group of issues. I refer to the large spectrum of challenges that we now associate with ecology—world population, food supply, pollution, dwindling supplies of nonrenewable natural resources, and so on. Even as I write these words, the newspapers are full of reports that the world is on the very edge of a chasm between food production and the growing population. A United Nations report issued in June of 1974 indicated that as many as 800 million people, nearly a quarter of the human race, are now suffering from malnutrition. World reserves of grain are lower than they have been for twenty years. A major crop failure would mean death for innumerable hungry people.

Mr. A. H. Boerma, General Director of the Food and Agriculture Organization of the United Nations, is calling upon the world to set aside 15% of the annual grain yield in a global food bank for emergency use to prevent starvation. North America is about the only region that has much surplus. The United States and Canada are to grain what Saudi Arabia is to oil. The sharp rise of prices in the grocery store puts a strain on most American budgets and is especially hard on the poor. Yet the moral responsibility of preventing starvation in other lands weighs heavily in the balance. By 1985 the Food and Agriculture Organization predicts an 85 million ton gap between grain production and world need. Those with money will get it unless a world bank is built up for the needy who may not have funds

The short-term strategy, then, is to build up grain reserves. The long-term solution is, first, to reduce population, and second, nearly as important, to increase the output of millions of peasant farmers around the globe. Recently it took 8 million Americans to produce 239 million tons of grain, while 364 million Indian farmers grew 105 million tons.[3]

And the race between population and food supply is only one among many warnings that the human race may be courting ecological disaster of unprecedented proportions. A team of highly respected scientists at the Massachusetts Institute of Technology has published a report in which they maintain that the world is headed for a major catastrophe within the next century unless some dangerous trends are reversed quickly.[4] If prevailing rates of increase in world population, food production, pollution, resource depletion, and industrialization continue, the limits to growth will be reached within a few generations. The consequence will be a sudden, sharp, and uncontrollable drop in world population and industrial capacity. These conclusions are buttressed with diagrams showing such complex interrelationships among ecological and economic factors that it took a computer to work them out. The pessimistic conclusions of *The Limits to Growth* are matched by those of a group of British scientists and philosophers who authored *A Blueprint for Survival*, which urges that growth be brought under control as soon as possible. These doomsday documents are highly controversial and subject to criticism from many angles. Nevertheless, they point vividly to a new dimension of the human predicament that must be faced by anyone concerned about the future of the world.

Even from this brief survey, two important lessons about our future come into view with startling clarity. (1) The whole world has become one interdependent system in which national and global issues blend into each other. (2) The concerns of justice and of ecology are inseparable. We do indeed live on Spaceship Earth, and we are all dependent on it. All we have for the foreseeable future is this planet with its limited resources and each other with all our fears and hopes. The magnificently beautiful picture that the astronauts on the moon took of the earth—that cloud-enswirled blue-green ball floating in space—is an image that must penetrate increasingly into our consciousness. Spaceship Earth is the most powerful symbol of our time. It must be a constant point of reference for everyone who wants to think responsibly about what the love of neighbor and the quest for justice mean for the present and future. The picture of earth made from the moon is a vivid image that impresses upon us anew what the psalmist taught long ago. "The earth is the LORD'S and the fulness thereof, the world and those who dwell therein." (Ps. 24:1) We are all one family under God, on God's earth, and no individual or nation has any right to superior status or privilege.

Let me illustrate the connection of nation with world and of ecology with justice by posing two problems. I invite the reader to think about them with me.

Problem One

Fact: The two greatest drains on the global environment today are rampant population growth in some of the underdeveloped countries and rising rates of consumption in the industrial nations. The increase in the global consumption of goods and services is due about equally to the population explosion and to the rise of individual affluence.[5]

Fact: With about 6% of the world's population, the United States uses from about 30% to 50% (estimates vary) of the world's raw materials.

Reflections: Rich nations and poor nations alike must be prepared to rethink some of their values and change their life-styles for the sake of all of us who are passengers on Spaceship Earth. When is enough enough? How many children are enough? How much income and how much consumption are enough? It is probably no easier for people in poorer countries to get used to the idea of having fewer children than it is for us to change our attitudes toward economic growth. Yet both are threatening the limits of the earth's capacity to sustain life. Do people have a right to consume all they can pay for? On the other hand, suppose industrial nations have fewer people but a higher level of *per capita* consumption. Is this not as legitimate a claim on world resources as that of extra mouths born in countries where population is outstripping food?

Question: Do you agree that if the developing nations are asked to reduce their population growth, the affluent nations should be willing to reduce their rates of consumption?

Problem Two

Fact: The average American or Canadian consumes about 2000 pounds of grain each year. In the poor countries, the average is about 400 pounds. (In North America, 150 pounds of grain are eaten directly in bread, pastries, and cereals; the rest is consumed indirectly in the form of meat, milk, and eggs. In the poor countries, most of the grain is eaten directly; little can be spared for conversion into animal protein.) Hence, the agricultural resources in land, fertilizer, and water required to support an average North American is five times that required for the average Indian, Nigerian, or Colombian.

Fact: Conversion of grain into meat is an inefficient way to get food value. It takes seven pounds or more of grain to produce one pound of beef, four pounds of grain for one pound of pork, and three pounds of grain to get one pound of chicken.

Fact: *Per capita* beef consumption in the United States has grown from 55 pounds in 1940 to 117 pounds in 1972.[6]

Reflection: If individuals in this country ate less meat, especially beef, this would free grain to be used directly to feed malnourished people. Of course, the money saved from not eating meat would have to be used to buy grain that would go to some hungry person. And reducing meat consumption would actually improve the diet of many Americans.

Question: Do you agree that North Americans should make an effort to reduce their consumption of beef for the sake of a more efficient use of available grains for the hungry nations of the world?

This book is mainly about values, what we treasure and what we live for. Already two basic values have come into view: (1) our attitude toward our nation and the needs and claims of other nations, especially the poorer ones, and (2) our attitudes toward individual consumption. Again, without presuming to have the right answers, let me raise some questions. Given the present ecological realities of rising consumption and dwindling natural resources, can we be content with a situation in which 1/16th of the world's people use up at least 1/3 of the world's nonrenewable raw materials? What is a fair share? Viewing our own nation alongside others, how are we to define the good life and the income it requires? For a family of four, when is enough enough? $15,000 a year? $20,000? $50,000? A million a year? The point is not that there is some level beyond which consumption becomes automatically immoral. There is no right or wrong as such about enjoying the benefits that money can provide. The issue is one of fairness in a world where wealth and privilege are distributed so unequally. The issue also involves ecological prudence: increasing consumption and population are beginning to press toward the biological limits of the earth.

In a time of rapid inflation and recession combined, most Americans do not feel very affluent. Nearly all of us are having budget problems these days. Nevertheless, by world standards, the majority of Americans are wealthy. Those families with incomes of $15,000 or more are in the upper half of the population of this country as far as money is concerned. Jesus told the rich young ruler that he should sell all his goods and distribute the money to the poor. Many Americans share the sadness of the wealthy young man as he turned away. We have worked hard for what we have. Much sacrifice and discipline have been necessary to get us where we are. We have finally achieved some comforts—a good house, a decent job, and the prospect of making life better for our children. Now we are told that we should feel guilty for having achieved the American dream. Why should we be prepared to give it up for the sake of the poor and the starving peoples who have never done a thing for us? Yet we can also understand that mothers and fathers in rural Appalachia or in Africa who have little food to give their children can hardly appreciate our dilemma. And it is unrealistic to suppose that the poor do not know what we have, or do not want it: communication has become cheap, universal, and intelligible even to the illiterate; and the ethic of acquisition we have instilled in ourselves we have also proclaimed to them. It is no wonder that there is a vague uneasiness and at times a deep troubling of the spirit throughout the land.

Let me move to the practical and immediate by indicating how the issues of wealth and justice come home to me as an individual. My family lives on the salary I make as a professor in a theological seminary. My income is modest compared to that of many other professionals with similar academic credentials and experience. Yet my family has more to spend than over half of all American families. In addition to my salary, which is a specific sum I can be sure of, I earn some additional money every year from lecture fees, preaching engagements, and even a little from book royalties. But since these vary from season to season, the income they produce cannot be counted on for regular budgetary purposes. For example, I may receive an invitation tomorrow to give a lecture in a month for which I may earn, say $100. This money is, in a sense, "extra." How do I decide what to do with it? I could, of course, use it in a thousand different ways to purchase something the family needs or at least wants. Or I can save it to pay for the college expenses of my three children or for security in old age for my wife and myself. But instead of spending this extra $100 on myself and family, I could also find a thousand ways to spend it to benefit some person, family, or group that has a desperate need for food, clothes, shelter, or medical care. I could send it to CARE with instructions to send a food package overseas to some area of famine. There are families in the city of Rochester who barely have enough to get by on from month to month. Newspaper stories tell of elderly people who are eating pet food. The possibilities for using this extra money are endless.

How can I enjoy a color TV set when there are children who lack even a crust of bread for their shriveling bodies and distended stomachs? How do I weigh this: should I give my income to develop the talent and intelligence of my children, or should I give it for other children who do not even have enough food and medical care to keep them alive and healthy? Every child is as precious to God as my child. How can I give my children cake when other children have no bread? What does the command to love one's neighbor equally with oneself mean in these circumstances? I do not argue that there are simple answers to the questions I have raised. I am troubled by the customary assumption that there are no limits whatsoever to the amount that a family may rightfully spend for its own necessities, wants, luxuries, and whims. In a world so full of need and creeping ever closer to the brink of ecological disaster, is there some point where we must finally say right out loud that ENOUGH IS ENOUGH?

My effort is to show that individual behavior is tied into global problems. I have tried to illustrate the kind of thinking we must be prepared to do if we are to deal with the problem of being morally responsible in a complicated world. To follow this out a bit will help us to see even more clearly how everything is connected to everything else. Suppose that a large number of affluent families in America made a conscious choice to restrict their consumption. What would the consequences be for the economy? What would and could be done with the excess over, say, $18,000 to $20,000 a year? Remember that either of these amounts is considerably higher than the income of more than half of American families. Would large sums suddenly invested in something other than consumer goods and services have potentially disastrous results for the stability of the economic system? Suppose that forty million Americans deliberately restricted their consumption of meat as a way of combatting world hunger. What would be the consequences for cattle-raisers, for companies and workers in the meat-packing and -distributing industry? What would happen throughout the whole economic system at home and abroad?

All we need do is recall some recent events to be reminded that we live in a complicated network of interrelated systems and forces. A change in one sector produces waves in some places and ripples nearly everywhere. In February of 1974 lines at the gas stations grew long and tempers grew short. Earlier the Arabs had imposed an oil embargo to protest our friendly policy toward Israel. The profits of the automobile manufacturers dropped sharply. The public started a rush to buy small cars. Workers in automobile factories were laid off. The tourist industry got scared. Makers of mobile homes, travel trailers, and other vehicles using gasoline faced financial ruin. Deaths from automobile accidents dropped 25% over a period of months, presumably because of reduced traffic and lower speed limits. Despite the continuing protests of environmentalists, Congress quickly passed legislation enabling construction to go forward on the Alaska pipeline. Demands were made that pollution control standards for auto emissions be relaxed in order to allow more efficient mileage from available gasoline. Meanwhile, the profits of the oil companies skyrocketed as prices at the gas pumps rose sharply. Word came from India that the increase in oil prices and in all the products made from oil threatened to bring an already shaky economy to its knees. When the oil embargo was lifted, the Arabs justified the rise in prices of crude oil by pointing out that inflation increased the cost of goods they had to buy from the industrial nations. Everything is connected to everything else. The whole world has become one giant trading center. Economic and political events in one part of the globe affect all the rest. Our hope for survival and prosperity depends on how well these vast systems and forces can work in harmony to achieve worthwhile human goals.

Another lesson about our world comes into view here. One of the problems in our world is the difficulty of getting reliable information about what affects vested interests. Were the oil companies taking advantage of a crisis to boost prices and profits, as some critics and some evidence seemed to show? By June we were told that gasoline supplies for the summer seemed ample, and the embargo was lifted—apparently for good. The oil companies argued that, after all, they only made about 2¢ a gallon profit, so what was all the fuss about? Don't blame us, they said, we are only passing along the higher costs of crude oil to the consumers. Besides, although these profits seem high, they are necessary to promote exploration so as to insure supplies for the future. It costs a lot of money to drill for oil and to build refineries these days. What was the truth of the matter? Were the oil companies taking advantage of us? Or were they just working very hard to keep the country running as their ads claimed, only wanting to make an honest and modest profit for their efforts? Again, commercials on TV told us over and over again how much the oil companies loved the environment. Exxon showed us pictures of hordes of fish swimming around their offshore drilling platforms. Meanwhile, Jack Anderson maintained that these same companies were being allowed to tone down, before its release, a government study which shows that oil spills have done great damage to the ocean.[7] How can we act responsibly if we can't even find out what the facts are?

The problem, however, is not simply getting the straight facts. It is also important to know how the facts and forces interact to form a total system of events. But to figure out how the world works calls for the kind of theoretical knowledge and practical know-how that only technical experts have—and even they do not always agree. I have already mentioned the pessimistic predictions of *The Limits to Growth*. The claim was that we were in danger from the consequences of exponential growth—the kind of increase where something keeps doubling over given periods of time. Critics, particularly economists, pounced on these doomsday predictions at once.[8] Their view was that what we had in this study was a classic example of "Garbage In" and "Garbage Out" from the computer. The MIT team, it was asserted, had taken the obvious mathematical fact that exponential growth cannot continue indefinitely in a finite world. Then they slanted the evidence so that the outcome was bound to sound as if catastrophe was ahead. They overestimated the threats of growth to the environment and underestimated our capacity to deal with them. The critics agreed that population growth does need to be curbed. But economic growth is not necessarily a villain if we manage it rightly. In particular, we can change the incentives to industry. We can make it costly to them to pollute and beneficial to them to find nonpolluting ways to produce their goods and dispose of their waste. Moreover, technology can find ways to substitute materials for depleted ones, discover ways to recycle what we already have, and so on. Hence, what we need is not to curb growth as such but to manage it prudently. How are ordinary citizens to decide for themselves when the experts don't agree on how the system works and on what should be done to keep it going?

Let me continue for a moment the debate over growth by showing how issues related to politics and values also enter. Many economists argue that it is unnecessary to curb economic growth, *if* we change our presently unwise policies that allow and encourage waste and pollution. They also argue that continued economic growth is the only way to overcome poverty. The percentage of the total wealth of the nation going to the poorest families and to the richest families has continued about the same over many years. Roughly, the upper 5% of the families have 20% of the income, while the poorest 20% get 5%. It would be relatively easy to redistribute wealth by political means, if those in power had any desire to. But our history gives little reason to suppose that significant income redistribution will come about politically.

In the fall of 1971, when Senator McGovern was beginning his campaign for the presidency, he proposed that all inheritances to a child over $500,000 should be taxed at 100%. He later modified the suggestion because it simply didn't go over very well. I thought it was a good idea. I knew I would never have that much to leave even one of my children, much less enough to give half a million to all three. I said to a young man in jest, "What? You mean I can only leave each of my children $500,000? How horrible!" To my surprise I found that he was seriously horrified at that notion. The likelihood that he will ever have half a million dollars to leave to anyone is about as great as that Ralph Nader will be the next president of General Motors. However, even though he would never have that kind of money, the man was shocked at the idea that the government would take away all above $500,000 for each child. Here we are talking about attitudes and beliefs. It is perhaps reasonable for individuals to be rewarded differently according to the contributions they make. But wealth is in a large measure the product of many people's work. Shouldn't there be a limit to what any person should be allowed to keep for purely private use? Elizabeth Taylor can command a million dollars for a single movie. But that million would not be available unless hundreds of thousands of ordinary people plunked down their three bucks at the box office. Why shouldn't the whole society share in such huge earnings? Henry Ford, it may be argued, deserved a sizable reward for his contribution to the automobile industry. The truth is, however, that he could not have made that fortune except for the workers who assembled his Fords and the millions who bought them. Did he deserve a billion dollar reward? The idea that the president of a huge corporation must have half a million dollars a year to provide incentive is incredible to me. Isn't there something at work here more than the money? What about justice? What is a fair share? When is enough enough? We are dealing here with values.

How, then, do we improve the lot of the poor, given the prevailing values and political facts of America today? Realism tells us that poverty can be relieved most easily by enlarging the economic pie. Then everybody can have a bigger slice. That way nobody objects very much. It is much harder to divide a smaller pie into more equal pieces. But suppose a reduction in economic growth becomes necessary for ecological reasons? Suppose we can't make the pie any bigger without risking environmental catastrophe? In this case, we can be sure that redistribution of wealth through political means will become a crucial issue in our society and will call for a decision from all of us.

It is time now to begin to sum up and to bring this chapter to an end. I have tried in a preliminary way to introduce some issues that this book will deal with. My basic concern is to throw some light on what it means to live as a morally responsible citizen in this complicated world. My analysis takes for granted that we live in a time of rapid technological and social change. It recognizes that necessary material goods and social services are provided by a vast network of interconnected organizations. These organizations now form a global system. We live in a world where social morality must recognize that planetary society is approaching the ecological limits of the earth. Put most succinctly, can we produce enough food and other material necessities for an expanding world population without polluting ourselves to death and without using up essential nonrenewable resources before we find substitutes or learn to recycle what we have? It is in such a world that the question of moral responsibility must be asked. My task in this book is to ask what it means to live out one's religious commitment in a complicated world. I want to make some suggestions as to how the churches might perceive their task in the years ahead.

It dawned on me in 1970 that my older daughter, then ten, would be the same age in the year 2000 as I was then—40 years old. At the beginning of the 21st century my children will be entering the midpoint of their lives. If for no other reason than that, it matters to me what the world will be like in another quarter of a century. I approach the questions in this book as a father, concerned about the future of my children. I write as an individual who wants some kind of satisfying life for himself—but one in keeping with being a morally responsible Christian. Finally, as a church member, I want to discover how the church may minister best to us and to our society.

Let me conclude this chapter by setting forth some of the convictions about the church and its ministry that are presupposed throughout the book. First of all, the primary function of the church is not to reform society. The first task of the church is to call people to religious faith, not to train them in social ethics. The church is not by original definition a social problem-solver. It has no special knowledge about how to change the institutions of society. The church is, first of all, a community which affirms a Creator and Redeemer who accepts us and loves us as we are with all our moral weakness. It celebrates the gospel of grace in the love and praise of God. The central focus of the church's message is on the ultimate issues of life and death. It calls people away from the idols they worship and calls them to center their lives upon God as the ultimate object of their trust and loyalty. The "good news" is not that the burden of managing the world is on our shoulders. The first note of the good news is that the God who created us loves us still. The Almighty wills and works for our salvation. The Bible invites us to live as children of God who find our highest joy and intended destiny in loving fellowship with each other and with our Creator. That is the center around which the life and witness of the church revolves.

Nevertheless, love of God and love of neighbor are inseparable dimensions of the Christian life. The Bible is unrestrained in its condemnation of those who profess to be religious but have no compassion for the needy. Amos tells us that God despises the sacred ceremonies of worshipers who are deaf to the cries of the downtrodden (Amos 5:21-24). Jesus says plainly that those who see the hungry and don't feed them, the prisoners and don't visit them, the naked and don't clothe them, and the homeless and don't offer them shelter are to be cast into the fire prepared for the devil and his angels (Matt. 25:31-46). Translated into the conditions of the present age, the message is clear. The total mission of God's people requires a corporate witness of the churches to the structures of society. My purpose, however, is not to convince Christians that they ought to change the world. If the Christians who read this book are committed to feeding the hungry, freeing the oppressed, and seeking a better life for everyone—that is, if they are Christians at all—they must wrestle with these issues.

In the second place, the churches do not have the kind of influence that would enable them to build a new society, even if they wanted to. They might have a powerful impact if they all agreed on some specific issue and threw their weight around in the political arena. Politicians do pay attention to churches where there are strong convictions likely to affect how people will vote. But the fact is that, generally speaking, most Christians do not see their responsibility as that of changing the political structures of the world or think of the church as an agent of social change. Nevertheless, there is a powerful fund of moral idealism among Christians. It needs to be mobilized and channeled into effective action on behalf of the suffering and oppressed. Christian faith does nourish compassion for the poor and the helpless.

In the third place, church members don't have significantly better ideas about what the future should be than people outside the churches. The political beliefs of Christians vary widely. Their social ideals tend to reflect the views of their race, region, economic class, age, and educational background. A few years ago the attitudes of white people on matters of race relations in the South could be fairly well predicted by examining a map which showed county by county the proportion of blacks to whites in the population. It appeared that where a person lived was a better indicator of beliefs about segregation than whether he or she belonged to a church. Besides, most of the people in America do belong to churches, so to say that the churches should change society is a bit like saying society should change itself. If by the church we mean the mainline denominations to which most Christians belong, they are part and parcel of the society in which they live. As social institutions they are more important as bulwarks of achieved social values than as instruments of change. Hence, whatever role our religious convictions tell us the churches *should* play in society, common sense compels us to be realists about the role mainline churches actually do play. Nevertheless, the mainline churches constantly generate within themselves smaller groups of highly motivated people who are at work on the frontiers of moral advance. A creative minority of Christians is committed to the achievement of ideals and goals not yet accepted in society generally. Wherever any evil is crushing out the lives of God's children, Christians have been among the first to take up the cause, whether the evil be slavery or segregation or war or hunger.

To conclude, let me simply say that to be a Christian in a complicated world a person must combine a warm heart and a cool head. By warm heart, I mean a deep Christian experience of the grace of God that expresses itself in a compassionate love for the world and all of its people. By cool head, I mean a hardheaded search to understand the way the world works. Let me borrow two phrases from Paul to express my meaning in a way that I hope does no violence to his intentions. He speaks of his fellow Jews as having a zeal for God but without enlightenment. And he speaks of knowledge without love as amounting to nothing. Zeal without knowledge is a warm heart without a cool head. Knowledge without love is a cool head without a warm heart. Both are essential to Christian discipleship in our time. Good intentions and warm piety are not enough. Sound judgment based on realistic understanding of the facts is also required. In order to add enlightenment to zeal, we must be prepared to spend some time examining the world in which we actually live. As best we can, we must also try to discern where we are probably headed. My aim is to try to provide some clues to the workings of present society and the new society that is emerging. The argument will unfold chapter by chapter. I will be leading up to a discussion of the mission of the church. The first step is to show that "the future is not what it used to be."

CHAPTER 2

The Future Is Not What It Used to Be

The difference between the world our grandparents knew and the world our grandchildren will live in staggers the imagination. My grandmother was born in 1865 at the end of the Civil War. America was still mostly rural and agricultural. The industrial era was just being born. The rapid growth of cities was barely getting underway. She died in 1950 in a society dominated by manufacturing industries. Huge urban centers were being rapidly surrounded by suburban housing developments and shopping centers. Five years before her death the world entered the atomic age. Mushroom clouds over Hiroshima and Nagasaki meant that a new era had begun. In other words, my grandmother's life began at the end of the rural, agricultural period. She lived through the triumph of the urban, industrial age. By the time she died, still another epoch was getting underway. This new age is being called by many names. I will refer to it as the megapolitan, cybernetic age. These terms require some explanation.

Begin by thinking about how things have changed in your own lifetime. If you are middle-aged or older, take a moment to remember how much in the world today is new since 1945. The list can grow long very rapidly—atomic energy generating plants, supersonic transport planes (SST), jet aircraft, oral contraceptives, tranquilizers, television, communication satellites, space vehicles that take men to the moon and cameras to Mars and beyond, hundreds of synthetic fabrics, the aerosol can, direct long-distance dialing, heart transplants, advanced computers, and so on and on. We have grown used to the threats of nuclear war, the population explosion, and ecological catastrophe. It is hard for me to remember how different things are today from the world I grew up in before World War II in rural Georgia. In my early childhood we had no running water, no indoor plumbing, no electricity. We cooked on a wood stove, kept our food in an ice box, and drew water from a well. We washed clothes by hand and boiled the dirtiest of them in a black washpot with a wood fire under it to get them clean. Many middle-aged people today have lived through such changes.

But we must push deeper to understand how this megapolitan, cybernetic society emerged. First of all, what do these words mean? Megapolitan refers to the clustering of large cities together to form huge belts of dense population. Three of these regions are especially important.[1] (1) Boswash. This is the string of cities along the Atlantic coast from Boston to Washington. It might better be called Portport. It would include everything between Portland, Maine, and Portsmouth, Virginia. By the year 2000 this area may contain 1/4 of the total population of the country, maybe about 80 million people. (2) Chipitts. This is the region around the Great Lakes from Chicago to Pittsburgh. It might extend north to Toronto, Canada and include Detroit, Cleveland, Toledo, Akron, Buffalo, and Rochester. The United States' portion of this may contain more than 1/8 of the population of the country by 2000, about 40 million people or more. (3) Sansan. This is the area along the Pacific coast from San Diego to Santa Barbara. In another 25 years this area may contain 1/16 of the population, about twenty million people. In all, half the people in the whole country, or even more, might live in these three megapolitan complexes. In addition to these huge urban strips, there will be smaller megapolitan regions in other parts of the country.

But this only tells us where most of us will be living. A more important question is *how* we will live. Also, we need to look at how the total life of the society will be organized to meet its needs and reach its goals. At this point I want to explain the other term I have already introduced. What is meant by a cybernetic society? Cybernetics comes from the Greek *kybernes*. It means steersman. It is related to the Latin *gubernator*, from which we get the word governor. Cybernetics, then, is the science of steering, of governing. It has to do with the ways we organize something in order to achieve a certain goal under changing circumstances. It deals with self-regulating, self-controlling, and self-correcting processes in machines, biological organisms, and social organizations. Anything that works by cybernetic principles can reach a desired goal or perform an assigned task despite changing conditions. The regulation of body temperature which keeps it at 98.6 degrees is a simple example of what I am talking about. A furnace that is operated automatically by a thermostat to keep a room at 68 degrees is nearly everybody's favorite instance of a cybernetic machine. I want to describe the society that is coming into being by using clues from cybernetics.

A cybernetic society would be self-guiding. It would have ways of achieving deliberately chosen goals. Ideally, in a democracy, everybody would have a part in choosing the goals. In fact, one of the basic problems facing our society will be to find ways to get all of us into the act. How can we make it possible for all people to have their say about what we should strive for as a nation and how we should go about getting the kind of society we want? I will be using the idea of a cybernetic society as a summing-up term. But not even this idea can suggest all the important features of the new world that is coming into being in our midst.

The cybernetic society will also be postindustrial.[2] A preindustrial society is engaged basically in taking things from the earth. Farming, fishing, mining, and cutting timber are the basic occupations. My grandparents on both sides were farmers. An industrial society continues to have people who till the soil and mine the earth for basic resources. But making products and selling them dominate economic life. My father was engaged in commerce and for a time was foreman in a textile mill that made hosiery. A postindustrial society, of course, must have farmers to raise food. It will also have many factory workers who manufacture products. The new feature, however, is that providing services occupies the work time of most employed people. I am a teacher.

> In 1900 most people lived in a rural area and made their living by farming, as my grandparents did.
>
> In 1940 the largest single group was by far the industrial workers who worked in factories, as my mother and father did.
>
> In 1960 the largest single group of workers was called by the census "professional, managerial, and technical people," like me and my wife who are teachers.
>
> By 1980 it is estimated that ⅔ of the work force will be engaged in providing services.

The service industries embrace trading, finance, insurance, real estate, transportation, entertainment, and communication, among others. Included are doctors, lawyers, TV repairmen, journalists, teachers, the clergy, sales clerks, barbers, professional athletes, and on and on. Are not most of you who are reading this page engaged in providing some service rather than helping to manufacture some product? We have already become the first service society in history. Over half of those employed are not involved in the production of tangible goods—food, clothing, housing, automobiles, and other such items. Providing services accounts for more than half of the gross national product of the country.

Another crucial feature of the cybernetic society is its reliance on knowledge.[3] In part, this means that more and more jobs require a course of study as preparation rather than training on the job. Some professions such as law and medicine have always required specialized training. But our grandparents lived in an age when the skills necessary to run the farm, work in the steel mill, keep the books in a store, or a thousand other things required little or no book learning. There are, of course, many such jobs today. But the trend is clear. In today's world more and more of the jobs with good pay and prestige require some technical knowledge and some understanding of theory. To be prepared, you need to go to school, read books, and learn from a teacher. We and our children know this quite well. The new jobs require the ability to apply a body of information to some practical situation. This is different from simply learning to use tools or operate machines. America will need increasing numbers of computer programmers, systems analysts, nurses, dieticians, medical technicians, psychiatric caseworkers, accountants, and so on through a long list. To get a good job today, it is more important than ever to know something as well as to be able to do something. In fact, knowledge has become our basic industry. The largest single occupation today is teaching. Teachers are needed to develop knowledge and to train people in applying it. By 1980 it is expected that every other dollar earned and spent will involve either producing or distributing ideas and information.

But we have still not touched on the most important feature of the emerging society. Every social order rests on knowledge and its transmission. Even the earliest agricultural societies had to teach children when and how to sow and reap. And of course, new ways of doing things, if they are to persist, must be passed along from generation to generation. The invention of the stirrup, the horse collar, the heavy plow, and clockwork —occurring between 500 and 1500—all represented a growth in practical knowledge, and all had powerful effects in transforming medieval society. Yet all these inventions came about as the result of practical experience. Someone facing a particular problem came up with a better way to do something mainly on the basis of trial and error. Beginning with the seventeenth century, science—especially physics—advanced rapidly; but invention was the result not of advances in science, but of advances in technology, and this was true well into the twentieth century. Henry Ford and the Wright brothers were more like traditional craftsmen than modern scientific researchers.

However, if we look to the future, the situation is different. What is decisive now is scientific ideas and technical theory. Such knowledge can be translated into many forms to produce solutions to practical problems. Some of the fastest growing industries today are electronics, computers, and pharmaceuticals. These, and new industries still to come along, will depend on the scientific discoveries of the twentieth century. The experts tell me that the computer depends on symbolic logic, a very technical subject. The development of computer science would be impossible apart from the mathematical theories of Alfred North Whitehead, Bertrand Russell, and John von Neumann.

Some of the inventions of previous centuries made it possible to replace human and animal muscles with machines. My grandfathers plowed their crops a row at a time with a mule. Today tractors cultivate large fields in a shorter time. But something different from this is shaping the world to come. We are even now in the age of electronics, the computer, and cybernetics. What is being replaced by machines today is not simply muscle power but brain power.[4] The new implements make it possible to process information and control operations that previously required the intervention of human thought. Using these systems it is possible to produce goods that are hardly touched by human hands. Such systems are able to receive information, make decisions, and send out signals that change or control complicated processes. A simple example is, of course, the thermostat. The furnace or air conditioner is turned on and off by a device that keeps the room at a constant temperature, regardless of what the weather is outside. The most spectacular instances are found in the recent space flights. Computers were used to make complicated calculations that guided the spacecraft to near pinpoint landings on the moon, a quarter of a million miles away.[5]

Computers are getting so smart it is scary. A host of jokes have already appeared reflecting our vague apprehensions that we may be replaced by machines with higher IQs than we have. Nearly everyone has heard the one about the Supercomputer that knows everything. The ultimate question is put to it. "Is there a God?" Supercomputer says, "Now there is!" My favorite story was told by Herman Kahn. A skeptic approaches Supercomputer. "If you know so much, tell me where my father is right now." Supercomputer says, "Your father is fishing off the coast of Cape Cod." The skeptic is elated. "That goes to show you're nothing but a big phoney. I happen to know that my father, Herman Schnell, is in San Diego." But Supercomputer has the last word. "It is true that Herman Schnell is in

San Diego, but your father is fishing off the coast of Cape Cod." Some experts believe that sooner or later computers can be made that feel as well as think. Everyone who has seen Stanley Kubrick's *2001: A Space Odyssey* will understand what is meant here.

Up to this point, we have been talking about mechanical and electronic technologies. We must move on to speak of "social technologies." By this I mean ideas and theories that can be used to solve problems where people as well as things are involved. The economists who advise President Ford about fighting recession and inflation base their suggestions on very complicated theories. Their models of how the economy works, their statistical charts, and their technical language leave us noneconomists mystified. We now face, and we will face in the future, multitudes of problems that we cannot possibly deal with apart from the help of experts in many fields. Finding alternative energy sources, combatting pollution, providing mass transit systems for cities—to mention just three current issues—require knowledge that only highly trained scientists and technicians possess. We are not nearly so sure as we were even a decade ago that the "social engineers" with their secret knowledge can successfully manage society and direct it toward desirable goals. Most of us are skeptical of the economic experts surrounding the president these days. There are some problems that are very hard to resolve no matter who is in charge and no matter how much expertise is around. It will be difficult to whip inflation and recession even with the help of the experts, but it is clear that we cannot solve these problems without them. The same holds of many of the other challenges the nation and the world face in the coming decades.

In short, there is a novel and glamorous language today. It speaks of operations research, systems analysis, technological forecasting, information theory, game theory, simulation techniques, decision theory, Delphi method, cross-impact matrix analysis, statistical time-series, stochastic models, linear programming, input-output economics, computer based command and control systems, and so on. All of these terms refer to ways of thinking which are used to understand and control some process that goes on in business, government, or in society generally. Name almost any area of modern life you can think of. It doesn't matter whether it involves nature or society. Somewhere there is a group of people thinking of ways to figure out what is going on and to improve the situation where possible. This holds whether we are thinking of how to grow more grain in the tropics, reduce the birth rate, control inflation, stimulate economic growth, get rid of tooth decay, provide better health care, find some way to turn garbage into a useful resource, reduce air pollution, win the next election, avoid war with Russia, develop human potential, extend the length of life, or find a cure for cancer. And all of these efforts to solve problems or to control some aspect of our economic, political, social, or educational life require the application of theoretical knowledge.

In business, in government, and in all the large organizations of our society a new form of power has been created. The importance of problem solving everywhere requires technical experts. They know the secret of making things work and we don't—and this makes them powerful. Moreover, knowledge-producing institutions of all sorts take on a new significance.[6] The universities will be especially important as the place where the problem-solving knowledge of the future will be created. Profit and nonprofit "think tanks," research institutes both public and private, the laboratories of industries, and many other institutions are at work providing the ideas and the inventions that will affect all of us tomorrow. I suspect that most of the people who read this book will have had some training in one or another of these knowledge-producing institutions. Many teach in a school or work in a research laboratory of some corporation. Others make use of ideas coming from these "knowledge factories" to do their work. More and more of us either are experts of some sort or depend on them in some way. Some of us who don't have any particular expertise may feel left out because our lives are being affected by something we cannot understand or control. It cannot be said too frequently that one of the fundamental challenges facing us lies right here. How can we make use of the knowledge of experts in solving our problems without creating an elite core of "social engineers" who plan our future for us without our advice or consent?

So far I have said that the cybernetic society is one that makes use of highly technical knowledge to solve problems and to invent better ways to get things done. It is also a society committed to managing change and guiding itself toward a more desirable future. This calls for intelligent planning which sets up consciously chosen goals and seeks ways of achieving them. All of this requires expertise of a highly technical sort. Solving problems and planning intelligently for the future requires knowledge and know-how that only advanced science and technology can give us. Future-oriented planning and social problemsolving based on expert knowledge are key features of the emerging cybernetic society.[7]

The first thing to keep in mind, then, is the centrality of problem-solving knowledge. Now a second main ingredient of the cybernetic society must be introduced: politics. By politics I mean the decisions we make as a people about how we want the society to be organized and managed. Government is the institution through which we decide what we want as a nation, what policies and rules we shall live by, and what goals we shall try to accomplish for ourselves. I have said that a cybernetic society is committed to managing change as best it can in order to achieve what it wants. As our society grows more complicated and interdependent, there are simply more decisions that we will have to make together. Moreover, in a time of rapid change we have to plan ahead. We have to ask, for example, where we will get our energy in 1980 and in 1990 and in 2000. This means that politics is very important in a cybernetic society. The political arena is where we make our decisions about what we want done here and now and about the goals we want to seek for the future. Government will inevitably be right in the center of our efforts to solve problems and plan for our future. To talk about politics is also to talk about power. We frequently disagree among ourselves about the laws we want passed and the policies we want our government to follow at home and abroad. The result is a struggle for power as competing individuals and groups try to elect officials who will support their interests against their opponents. Conflicts are inevitable as we seek to solve our problems and plan our future.

Three reasons can be given for the view that decision making in the political arena will be a crucial feature of the emerging society.[8]

1. The growing impact and expense of technology requires governmental intervention. The recent debate over the supersonic transport plane is an illustration of my point. Will the environment be damaged by hundreds of these aircraft flying at high altitudes and throwing their exhausts into the stratosphere? Why should a farmer in Iowa be taxed to build an airplane in which he will never ride? Should the average citizen approve of government support for the SST just so an affluent New York businessman can save a few hours flying to London? Why shouldn't private enterprise provide the money? Should corporations come running to Washington for help with a big project like this when they usually want the government to leave them alone? Many such issues face us.

The problems become more acute when we take a long-range look. Technology creates an impact for future good or ill. Hence, support of technology cannot be dependent on what the public wants now. Nevertheless, we can only choose among alternatives presently available. Ordinary citizens like ourselves do not know enough about future technological innovation to vote today with ballots or with dollars in the market. A problem arises because of the future planning required. A democratic government responds to the needs and demands of the present electorate, yet the Congress and the president make decisions that will have an impact on a generation of voters in the future.

2. America is becoming a homogeneous society. Increasingly issues in one part of the economy affect *all* our citizens. And when a problem confronts very large numbers of people, government must act. There are more of us. We live closer together. We are more dependent on each other. If truck drivers strike, the whole economy comes to a halt. If farmers decide to raise fewer cattle, the consequences touch all of us. The result

is that more decisions have to be made in the public arena of political debate. Since the days of Franklin Roosevelt, the federal government has been strongly committed to regulating the economy in order to promote prosperity. Congress and the president are playing a larger role than ever in promoting the general social well-being of all citizens. Laws have been passed recently, for example, to protect money that working people have invested in pensions. Action has been taken to protect the civil rights of black people and to guarantee women equal employment opportunities. We will need to cast our votes at the ballot box to help decide how public policy should be formulated on many issues like this. Let me just list some areas that will require government action and planning: rejuvenating the centers of big cities, providing mass transportation systems, controlling pollution, maintaining open spaces and recreational areas, taking care of future energy needs, making health care available to all.

3. A growing number of organizations and groups demand action to protect their rights. For years the government has listened to big business, labor unions, and farmers. Doctors have exerted political influence through the American Medical Association. Other groups have had their lobbies. But the list is rapidly growing. Recently pressures have been brought to bear on Congress and the president by blacks, the elderly, women, consumers, public employees, welfare mothers, the poor, atheists, militant students, homosexuals, Indians, and minorities of all sorts. Everybody wants to be heard. That is everybody's right in a democracy.

A third and final dimension of the cybernetic society must be mentioned briefly: the importance of values and goals. What problems shall we try to solve? Shall we invest more billions in ventures into space? Or should we try to make the cities livable? Shall we reduce the defense budget and use more of our national income to meet social needs at home like housing and medical care? We have said that in a time of rapid change, planning for the future is crucial. All institutions, both public and private, are looking ahead and asking what they should do now in order to achieve some desired goal. Planning for the future requires us to make decisions about what we want and how we shall go about getting it. It raises the questions of the ends to be sought and the means to be used in attaining them.

In the nation as a whole, the problem is that the values and goals of one group conflict with those of other groups. Oil companies wanted the Alaskan pipeline built. Environmentalists objected and wanted to find other ways to get the oil transported. The "energy crisis" of 1974 finally persuaded Congress to allow the pipeline. Liberals want more public services and more social welfare legislation. Conservatives want to hold government spending and taxes down. For some, busing is acceptable as a way to achieve racial integration. For others, the neighborhood schools are more important than having whites and blacks educated together. By helping people better understand the costs, the benefits, and the consequences of one choice over another, it may be possible to clarify what is involved for everybody. This will not, of course, eliminate conflicts between the priorities that different groups have. Since more and more issues will be decided by political means, we should be prepared for a continuing series of power struggles and inevitable compromises as the nation seeks to chart its future course. To sum up, the future of our society depends on the interactions among the three factors I have discussed. Diagrammed, it looks something like this:

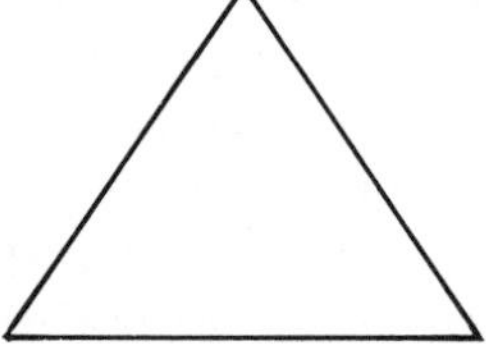

Many of our problems will have a technical dimension that requires expert knowledge and advance planning. But first, decisions must be made about which problems we want to tackle and what goals we want to strive for. This takes us into the area of politics where groups struggle for power, attempting to get their priorities high on the list. Already we have introduced the matter of values and preferences. Problem solving, decision making, and goal setting all involve and lead to each other. To put it differently, knowledge, politics, and values are mutually interdependent. A change in any one of these areas leads to changes or at least possible changes in the other two. All three have to be taken into account separately and together if we are to understand how our society works and how it changes.

It is clear why I have suggested that there are similarities between a cybernetic machine and a social organization. The world is made up of many kinds of systems,[9] and systems are made up of parts that work together to carry out some function or achieve some goal. In ordinary conversation we speak of the heating system in a house, the respiratory system in the body, and the family as a social system in a society. "Systems theorists" study every type of system they can to see if there are features that they all have in common. They believe that there are similarities between a mechanical system (an automobile, for example) and a social organization (the government, for example). Moreover, some systems are cybernetic. This means they have the ability to regulate themselves despite changing conditions. They can carry out their job or reach their goal under changing circumstances. A cybernetic torpedo fired from a submarine will change course in order to hit a moving target. No matter which direction the ship turns, the torpedo will correct its aim and go right to its mark. A machine, an animal, a person, and a society are all systems. By identifying the principles common to all of them, it is possible to increase our understanding of complicated systems by comparing them with simpler ones. Obviously there are vast differences between a torpedo, a cat, a human being, and a society. Still, by putting together the similarities and the differences between various kinds of systems or organizations, we can gain better ideas of how a society works and of what must be done to change it in desirable ways.[10]

Our interest here is in what a cybernetic society is like, so let us look at a social organization rather than at a mechanical system. Imagine a group of people who have been given the task of designing a heating system for a house they will inhabit. How shall they go about the job? What factors must they take into account in order to succeed? My imagination tells me that three different points of view would come to the surface right away. One group would insist that problem-solving knowledge is the basic requirement. Know-how is needed to design the furnace and the other equipment. In addition, expertise is required to organize work teams, to figure out ways the group can make decisions, and to determine where to set the thermostat. Setting the thermostat requires knowledge about what is best for health. Somebody around should be an expert in "group dynamics" in order to reach a compromise between those who want the house kept at a cool and ecologically sane 68 degrees and those who insist on a warm, cozy 72 degrees. Finally, the group needs to know which is the best energy source for heating in the face of dwindling fuel supplies and the dangers of pollution. In other words, this segment of the crew would claim that the best hope for success lies in the ability of the group to gain enough knowledge about people and furnace building in order to solve all the problems they will face.

Others would insist that to start with knowledge is to make a fatal move. The fundamental fact about any group, they would say, is that there are different self-interests within it that put people in conflict. Where no agreement can be reached, the strong take over. The values of those who take control of decision making will determine what kind of heating system is built and where the thermostat is to be set. It will not much matter what the so-called disinterested experts work out and tell us is best. The strong can hire their own experts for a price. Scientists, engineers and experts of all sorts will follow the money. The main problem is to deal with the political questions and the problem of power. A way must be found to allow the majority to rule without infringing on the rights of minorities. Until power is fairly distributed and the problems of leadership and decision making are worked out, there will be no peace. And there will be no progress toward getting a heating system built. Meanwhile, the strong, the resourceful, and the rich will get their way. The poor, the weak, and the minorities will be pushed into a cold corner where they cannot even see much less touch the thermostat.

Finally, there is a third point of view. This segment would argue that the basic thing is really "the value question." After all, they would say, knowledge is used to create means to satisfy desires. Decisions are made in the light of what the group's goals are. If there were no want or need for a heating system, there would be no project in the first place. If the group were highly committed to a project, they could put aside their differences and work together. But right now there is no clear harmony on a goal: everyone in the group is concerned primarily about getting heat for himself or herself and doesn't care about the rest. Some prefer to set the thermostat at 60 degrees to conserve natural resources and reduce pollution. Others hate technology and want to go back to an old wood fireplace. Some idealists in the group are bound to say, "We have to decide what kind of world we really want and create life-styles that fully develop 'human potential.' What is called for really is a 'new consciousness.' Only when we get our values straight will we be able to create a political system that will treat everybody fairly and put knowledge to work on the important problems."

Which of these groups is right? Each point of view is right in what it includes but wrong to the extent that it leaves out what the other two are saying. I have, of course, contrived the parable to make an obvious point. A well-adjusted cybernetic organization must have harmonious interaction among all three: problem solving (knowledge), decision making (politics), and goal setting (values). The example I have used here is a simple one. Nevertheless, the fact that each one of these elements depends on and involves the other two holds true for society as a whole.

I made up the parable about the group assigned to build a furnace, but the characters are taken from real life. Suppose we ask, "What's wrong with the world today, and what must we do to make things right?" Three types of answers tend to be forthcoming. One group says our problems are caused by the rapid changes brought about by science and technology. The invention of nuclear weapons puts the world under the threat of "the Bomb." Improved medical care in the poor countries has kept people alive who otherwise would have died in infancy. Now they grow up to reach child-bearing age. The absence of birth control measures is allowing populations to explode with horrifying speed. Cars, airplanes, and industries use up oil at such enormous rates that sooner or later we are bound to run out. So the argument goes. What is the answer? Usually those who give this diagnosis urge that our only hope is more science, more technology, more expert knowledge to solve the problems of war, population, hunger, pollution, energy shortages, and so on. John Platt in a famous article[11] and Buckminster Fuller in his book *Utopia or Oblivion*[12] represent this point of view. Some of the speeches of President John Kennedy also argued this way. We have gone beyond the debates between the capitalists and the socialists. What we need today, he said, is not passionate commitment to some ideology but cool technical expertise to manage a complicated economy. And, in his administration, faith in the experts to solve our problems at home and abroad was very strong.

A second group will say that the basic problem is not technological but political. The trouble is that some groups have too much money and too much power. Others have too little. The result is that the strong take advantage of the weak. Those who take this line will point out that the concentration of economic power has increased. In 1949 the richest 1% of the population owned 21% of the wealth. Today the richest 1% owns nearly 40% of the wealth. Income distribution has not changed for a generation. Rich people and huge corporations have too much political power and manage to get laws passed that benefit them. Moreover, they are able to influence foreign policy so that our military, economic, and food aid goes to countries where multinational corporations have the most likelihood of making profits. What is the answer? Again the prescription is in keeping with the diagnosis of the illness. A reform movement is needed that will unite the majority of low and middle income people in this country into a political coalition that can elect a Congress and a president who will change the system. The power of the huge corporations would be curbed. Income would be redistributed. Inequalities of wealth, privilege, and opportunity would be overcome. Foreign policies would be formulated to serve the best interests of the whole country and of oppressed peoples everywhere. In their book *A Populist Manifesto*, Jack Newfield and Jeff Greenfield spell out a detailed program of political reform along these lines.[13]

A third group would focus on our beliefs, our attitudes, and our values. What is our puoblem? We are too committed to the pursuit of things, money, success, status, and privilege. We value competition too highly, cooperation too little. We put too high a premium on those things we can buy for ourselves as individuals while resenting the taxes which provide public goods such as mass transit, schools, social security, and welfare but which do not directly benefit us. Little girls are taught to be sweet, passive, and to love having babies and keeping house. Little boys are taught to be tough, aggressive, and to prepare themselves to run the world while their wives stay home to rock the cradle. Whites think they are superior to blacks and try to keep them down. Blacks are resentful and tend to blame all their failures on oppression by whites. We have an obsession with growth. Bigger is better. Our football team, our nation, our whatever must be number one. Winning is all that matters. Nice guys finish last. On and on the arguments go. The claim that our problem lies basically in mistaken beliefs, wrong attitudes, unworthy motivations, and generally mixed-up values takes many forms. So does the prescription. All of them agree, however, that we need more than science and technology, more than political reform: what we need is a conversion of the total self in which we get our heads and hearts straightened out. Charles Reich in *The Greening of America* offers us a version of the "new consciousness" that he thinks we need.[14] Philip Slater in *The Pursuit of Loneliness*[15] and Theodore Roszak in *The Making of a Counter Culture*[16] give us similar prescriptions for the good life.

What I have been suggesting can be put under two headings.

(1) Ideas taken from cybernetics can help us understand how our society actually works at present. (2) They can also help us get some understanding of what must happen in the future if desirable change is to come about. In both cases we have to talk about the way the three factors I have mentioned interact with each other. Change in society can start in any of these three areas. A new invention can set off a chain reaction of changes all through society. The appearance of the automobile, for example, has affected everything from dating customs to the way suburban housing developments are laid out. In the days of Franklin D. Roosevelt a new political activism developed in response to the Depression. Since that time the government has been expected to take decisive action to promote prosperity and social welfare in areas where Congress and the president previously took a hands-off attitude. Finally, we only have to think for a moment to realize how changing values can affect the way we live. Just think of the attitudes relating to sex, marriage, divorce, and the rights and role of women. Many of us remember how shocked we were when Rhett Butler uttered the word *damn* in the movie *Gone with the Wind*. Even such innocuous words as *virgin* and *seduce* were not introduced into movies until 1953 (in *The Moon Is Blue*). Today, however, X-rated films, coed dormitories, naked men in *Playgirl* and naked women in *Playboy* are so much a part of the scene that we forget how recently it has all come about.

It would not seem profitable, then, to look for some *one* place where social change always begins. The way a society evolves as it moves into the future is a complicated affair. It seems best to recognize that change can begin with a new invention or the discovery of a better way to solve some problem. It can begin with a political change as new groups with different ideas and goals come into power. And it can begin with a change in what people believe is desirable or right or good. But wherever it begins, change in one area always produces equally great changes in the other two.

One principle, however, can be stated about change, regardless of its causes or consequences. Individuals and groups are likely to change only when they feel either a powerful need or a powerful threat. Later on I will develop the idea that life comes with a built-in drive for fulfillment, for satisfaction and enjoyment, for security and happiness. When something blocks the fulfillment of our needs or when there is a chance of somehow improving our situation, then we will be open to people, ideas, ideals, and strategies that promise change. When we are happy with the way things are, then we are likely to resist change. When present arrangements in society enable us to get what we need and want, we will probably try to keep everything as it is.

We are likely to oppose new inventions or ways of solving problems if they upset what we are accustomed to and like. We will vote against or otherwise fight to keep groups from getting political power if what they will do threatens our advantage. We will be tempted to call ideas, attitudes, and values different from ours bad or dangerous or sinful.

This, of course, is too simple; real life is more complex than this. But the general rule does seem to hold. People are open to change when they feel oppressed, frustrated, or threatened. They will resist change if it is likely to oppress, frustrate, or threaten them. The general formula can be put simply: basic changes in individual lives and in society occur when a threat, need, or want is felt and a positive alternative promises relief. Illustrations of this formula abound at every level of life. People responded well to the lowering of speed limits to 55 mph when they thought it might save scarce and expensive gasoline. The result was a 25% reduction in highway fatalities. People had been told for years that slowing down would save lives, but this advice had little effect. The point is that most people did not feel personally threatened by large auto-death statistics and so there was little inducement to slow down; but when people paid drastically higher prices for gas, and were threatened with having no gas, they took the threats to their money and mobility seriously, and slowed down. From this, another element of the general formula is clear. It is important that threats and benefits be felt directly. The more remote the consequences, the more startling they have to be to motivate change.

Something like this formula for change in attitudes and behavior was the assumption underlying the revivalist preaching

I heard in my youth. The sinner is under the threat of hellfire and damnation. The good news is that salvation is possible through the saving work of Christ which offers hope and heaven. The message was that people had a choice: they could continue to live in sin and be subject to the wrath of God here and hereafter; or they could accept Christ, live in obedience to his commands, and be rewarded with everlasting life. Much of what the Old Testament prophets and what Jesus and his New Testament apostles taught assumes this pattern. Save yourself from the threat of destruction by meeting the demand that leads to salvation.

Throughout this book I will be talking about the importance of having a vision of future possibilities for which we can hope and work. My assumption is always that such goals are impotent unless they offer relief from bondage and danger and unless they promise freedom and fulfillment. Many of us do feel threatened today. We look for a vision that is liberating and hopeful. We are at a critical point of transition from one era to another. This is true for the world as well as for the nation. There is a general malaise, and a general anxiety about the future. The perils and the promises are equally great. My purpose is to challenge individuals and churches to look upon the perils as a challenge which calls for a hopeful vision of the future. What we need are realistic goals that will inspire us to act. If we are to avoid the perils and realize the promises of the coming decades, vision and a plan of action are essential. What role can the church play? What can individuals do? These are the questions I hope to throw some light on.

At the close of this chapter I want to state clearly a theme that will more and more come into the center of attention in succeeding pages. The church is not equipped to deal with the scientific and technical issues that will be central in the next two or three decades. Neither is its primary function to be found in the arena of political decision making or the struggle for power between competing social groups. Though the witness and work of the church have important implications for each of these areas, its first priority is not there. What the church *is* equipped to do in the light of its history and faith is to confront the hard facts of the present with the ideal possibilities of the future. To project realistic goals for the society of the future in both its national and global dimensions, to nourish a consciousness embodying the ideas, ideals, and life-styles appropriate to the emerging society—these define basic tasks to which the public ministry of the church should be directed.

A related function is to provide a laboratory of reflection in which Christian believers can learn to relate the goals and values of a Christian outlook to the secular sphere in which they function in daily life. The church's task, seen in this light, is twofold: (1) to elaborate a vision of earthly society modeled on the Kingdom which Jesus inaugurated, and to describe this model in the common language of today, and (2) to help Christian citizens discover ways of living which will bring their vision to reality.

In order to accomplish these tasks, individuals and churches will need the gift of what I shall call visionary reason. This idea will be developed further in a later chapter. Briefly put, by visionary reason I mean the creative imagination God gave us to guide our lives toward desirable goals in pursuit of the good life. Visionary reason is the gift that the prophet Joel says the Spirit will pour out on us in the latter days.

> And it shall come to pass afterward,
> that I will pour out my spirit on all flesh;
> your sons and your daughters shall prophesy,
> your old men shall dream dreams,
> and your young men shall see visions.
> Even upon the menservants and maidservants
> in those days, I will pour out my spirit. (Joel 2:28-29)

This gift to dream dreams is needed desperately today. We can have it if we seek it.

The claim of this chapter has been that the forces that are creating the society of tomorrow may be managed for the benefit of all by a cybernetic society democratically planned. The next chapter has to do with the threats and promises posed by our increasing dependence on technological reason. Another chapter will contend that technological reason needs to be under the direction of visionary reason. The final section calls the church to be a nourisher of Christian ideals for the society of tomorrow. Visions of the human future inspired by Biblical hope are a key both to the prophetic critique of false gods and to designing strategies for a good and growing life for all God's children.

CHAPTER 3

Technology: Master or Servant?

According to a medieval legend the Rabbi of Prague once molded a statue of clay and brought it to life by placing the sacred and unspoken name of Almighty God on its forehead. The man-made god increased in size and ability to accomplish great tasks. All was fine at first. But the people began to fear it as it continued to grow. They erased the first letter of the sacred name from its forehead, and it died. Numerous commentators have seized upon this ancient story as a parable of our own times. As the power of technology grows, its earlier promise seems to many to be turning into a threat. Can technology save us, or do we need to be saved from it? Should we rejoice in or be frightened by the acceleration of those forces which created our technological civilization? The rapid expansion of scientific knowledge and practical know-how are putting unprecedented powers in human hands to bless or to curse the earth. Are the optimists right in claiming that technology can provide solutions to major world problems? Or are the pessimists right in protesting that technology itself is a major cause of potential catastrophe?

The principal charge of the pessimists[1] is not that some particular technological developments will ruin us. Actually, Jacques Ellul, one of the most influential of them, is an optimist on this point. He maintains that the individual problems caused by technology can be cured by more technology. The population explosion and pollution are offered as examples of troubles that can be remedied in this way. His charge goes much deeper. So does that of the other pessimists. Their claim is that the real enemy is *technological reason* itself. This complaint has profound implications for the future of the human race. What do the pessimists mean by technological reason? Why is it such a danger?

The pessimists take a long historical view. They see the technological way of reasoning and of solving problems as one of the great forces that have shaped the modern world. And increasingly, these forces have called into question the belief that we are made in the image of God. The faith that we live in a world of moral laws ordained by a sovereign creator has weakened. Atheist philosophies of various types have become increasingly common. A principal one, for example, is positivism. This is the view that only what can be examined by the senses with the help of scientific methods is real. The result is that human beings are reduced to the level of robots. People are just one among the many phenomena that make up the physical world. We, like stones and worms, are encased in a network of material forces completely devoid of intrinsic spiritual meanings. People are complicated machines in a neutral world of facts. Moral values are nothing more than human inventions. Moreover, there is no evidence or need for a creator. In short, in a world without God or values, people are reduced to things. Hand in hand with such a philosophy, confidence in technological reason has come to reign supreme in our world. And the pessimists dislike technology precisely for its philosophy—its materialism.

According to the pessimists, science, industry, and bureaucracy—as well as technology—illustrate this threat to humanity.

1. *Science:* For three centuries, science seemed to imply that the world is a giant machine. A machine just does what it does. It has no purposes of its own, no aims, no feelings. It is just matter in motion. Its movements can be charted in exact mathematical laws to which there appear to be no exceptions. Despite this machine-universe view, many still argued for the existence of God. After all, the only machines we know about were created by a designer. Just as a watch requires a watchmaker, so the world machine calls for a divine worldmaker.

Again, one might argue that human beings are free, moral agents and not machines. Like the creator, they too stand outside the realm of physical reality with its machinelike laws. So, belief in God and in human freedom and dignity persisted. But science continued to grow in its power to describe the world and its laws. Skepticism grew. The Bible indicates that the world was created a few thousand years ago in a short time by a direct act of God. Geology proved that belief to be false. Miracles seemed impossible. Faith in them appeared to be a product of religious imagination run wild. Atheism came to be seen by more people as the religion of the future. Some enthusiasts claimed that ultimately everything human could be explained completely in terms of the laws of physics and chemistry. Darwin offered evidence that human beings had evolved from lower animal species. Later scientists concluded that life itself sprang from nonliving matter by purely natural processes. The final blows to human dignity seemed to have been delivered. Thus, science raised the basic question of modern philosophy. What is the place of persons and their quest for meaning in a world viewed as a purposeless network of causes and effects?

2. *Technology:* Both Jacques Ellul and Lewis Mumford see the clock as the epitome of machine design. It is the prototype of all those mechanical arrangements to which humanity would increasingly be subjected. A long time was required to design a machine that could measure time accurately. The perfection of clockwork in the 14th century was a major triumph of mechanical intelligence. The perfected clock was a superb example of rational design, efficiency, organization, and mathematical order. The first known reference to the universe as a machine was made in 1382.[2] In the 17th century the principles of physics and of planetary motion were worked out, and clockwork provided an apt analogy for the whole natural universe. Moreover, the clock was used to determine when to work, when to eat, when to sleep, and when to worship. Living by the clock replaced living by the organic rhythms of the body and of nature. For many of the pessimists, this symbolizes the beginning of a trend which leads gradually to a time when the whole of life will be mechanized in clockwork fashion.

3. *Industry:* The assembly line carries the clockwork principle into the heart of the work life. Workers are given highly specialized tasks to perform repeatedly throughout the day. The efficiency expert is called in to show how human muscle and mind can achieve the most work with the least effort and in the least time. Other experts are called in to examine every detail of the work process. They look for ways to keep the worker content amid the inevitable boredom and monotony of the assembly line. The Charlie Chaplin movie *Modern Times* (1934) illustrates the effect of all this in comic fashion. It shows an assembly-line worker after he leaves the factory. He is unable to break out of the mechanical movements that were required of him all day on the job.

4. *Bureaucracy:* In business, government, education, and other large organizations, we can see something similar happening. A highly specialized division of labor is everywhere in evidence. Large numbers of people are organized like a pyramid in which everybody has a boss just above him or her. Final authority is lodged at the top of the pyramid. Efficiency is the goal. Rational calculation is the means to achieve it. Each person is assigned a routine task. Everyone works in conformity with a set of detailed regulations. The aim is to make the whole enterprise work as smoothly as possible, just like clockwork. Bureaucracies seek to reduce all transactions to some standard routine. This leads to the "red tape" that confronts us everywhere. We are all subject to endless rules, regulations, procedures, licenses, permits, and so on, from which there is little escape. We face it in school, at the office, in the factory, in the hospital, and, most of all, in the government. Hence, persons are fragmented into all the numerous roles they play as workers and citizens.

Viewed in this way, science, technology, industry, and bureaucracy have all contributed to the mechanization of life. The physical world is a machine. People are made into robots. That is the final result of technological reason. So say the pessimists. The novelists, poets, philosophers, and theologians among them have a common complaint: modern society reduces human beings to a cog in the social machine.

But over against this fear has been an equally powerful faith. For the optimists, science and technology are not the architects of a fate worse than death. They are our best hope for overcoming misery and promoting happiness.[3] This faith has many ingredients. One is the belief in progress.[4] The expectation that life gets better for most people as time passes has been widespread since the 18th century.[5] A basic source of the confidence in progress is the Biblical idea that the Kingdom of God will come at the end of time. In its secular version, this hope means that life will progressively get better on earth.[6] Another root of the idea of progress is the aphorism of Francis Bacon that "knowledge is power." Learning the secret of things gives us power over them. The philosophers of the Enlightenment taught that reason can provide an understanding of nature and its laws. Growth in knowledge will lead to improvements in material standards of living. These philosophers also believed that people were basically virtuous; they supposed that improved standards of living, and habits rationally modified by knowledge, would lead to gradually rising moral standards in society. These beliefs have shaped us all. But belief in progress has been badly shaken by the catastrophes of the 20th century. The sinking of the *Titanic* in 1912 was symbolic of the death of all those rosy hopes that gradually social ills would be overcome and prosperity and justice would reign everywhere. World War I, the Great Depression, the rise of Hitler, the slaughter of millions of Jews, World War II, and the threat of atomic annihilation have all made it much more difficult to believe that time will bring nothing but good. Nevertheless, Americans still have great faith that life can be made better. We still have strong hopes that problems can be solved.

The promise of science and technology has been one major support of the belief in progress. For more than a thousand years a steadily rising stream of inventions has been transforming the way we live. Optimists, like Buckminster Fuller[7] and Glenn Seaborg,[8] claim that the challenges of the future can be met by increasing our scientific and technological abilities. Fuller puts his hope in the genius of engineers like himself. They could make the world a success if politicians and their obsolete ideas were not in the way. Engineers could design a global plan that would integrate the world's economies and provide material plenty for all. Seaborg holds out the promise that technology, especially that associated with nuclear power, is our best resource. Wisely used, our human powers can provide global prosperity, make war obsolete, and usher in a new day of harmony and worldwide cooperation.

It would be a mistake, however, to focus only on technologies that help us deal with nature. Other kinds of knowledge also bring power. A new breed of futurists has recently appeared. I refer to the theorists, planners, forecasters, and analysts who make a vocation of studying the future. The more enthusiastic among them believe that we can manage society as well as control nature. With the help of computers and new methods of collecting vast amounts of information, we can chart the probable consequences of any policy choice we make today.[9] Equally utopian are the proponents of "operant conditioning" (B. F. Skinner) and similar conceptions. They hold out the hope that such techniques can be used to design a whole society that will be happy, productive, peaceful, and secure.[10] Most far out of all are those who propose technologies that affect the human organism itself in a direct way: cloning (a process to reproduce genetically identical copies of a person), cryonics (freezing bodies at death for later revival when science has advanced sufficiently), and eugenics (designing genetically a superior organism). The increasing sophistication of problem-solving reason is our best hope for achieving a peaceful, prosperous, happy, secure world. So runs the claim of the optimists.

In today's society, then, fear and faith confront each other. Who is closer to the truth, the pessimists or the optimists? The rest of this chapter will sort out these contradictory claims. A balanced view will include the valid elements of both sides. Much of what the pessimists and the optimists say is based on their choice of a standard example of what technology really is and does. The symbol used by the pessimists is the clock. A clock breaks up the flow of natural time as measured by the organic rhythms of the body and of nature. It quantifies time and divides it into precise moments of identical duration.

Clockwork is a marvel of rational order and efficiency. When it is used to regulate human life, people eat, sleep, work, rest, rise, retire, go, come, worship, and even make love when it is "time to." Readings on a dial tell us when to do what. Hence, a control is set up which subjects the organic urges and free choices of the natural self to a pattern imposed from without by a machine. Technological pessimists see this simple mechanical invention as the forerunner of all the machines and organizations that make up urban, industrialized, bureaucratic society. Human beings are increasingly subject to extensions of the clockwork principle in the name of order, efficiency, and problem solving.

A *New York Times* article gives us a good example of what the pessimists have in mind.[11] Leonard Levin reports that there are no light switches in the new World Trade Center in New York City. If someone wants to work late in this huge building on Tuesday night, the Port Authority must be notified by Monday noon. The lights are turned on and off by computers. Levin comments that we mortals are expected to conform to schedule in giving birth to an idea. Otherwise, we may finish by candlelight. Should we blame technology for this? Are not people —the designers—responsible for omitting light switches and turning the job over to computers? Yes, of course. But the pessimists argue that we are so under the spell of efficiency that we go on creating more of these clockwork systems that force us to comply with their demands. Somehow the logic dictated by technological reason is thought to be best. So we plunge ahead in such a daze that we fail to see where all this is taking us.

This leads us to the next point. As long as technological reason is limited in its scope, no great problems arise. But technologies begin to link up with one another. They spread geographically. They increase in number and kind. More and more they touch each other in ways that require their integration in a more comprehensive harmony. In short, a system begins to be created that grows and grows. A little clockwork system here, another one there, and still a third yonder expand and mesh with each other. Larger and larger social organizations emerge. Order and efficiency require their unification into more and more inclusive systems. Finally, the network becomes so interwoven that the total system of technologies and social organizations begins to take on a force and a direction of its own. As the system expands, the room left for human spontaneity, freedom, and choice contracts. To operate all these systems and to invent still new ones to solve problems created by the old ones requires a growing core of experts. No one can question their actions because no one understands the connections of the systems these experts are working on; they alone possess the knowledge that keeps the machines, the organizations, and the people working together. And because increasing numbers of decisions are being made by machines, people begin to feel incapable of making decisions on their own. Hence, when the clockwork principle is extended until it includes absolutely everything, people will have ceased to be human. In the vision of Roderick Seidenberg, technological reason will continue to organize every aspect of life until the one best way to do everything has been found. The distant future, then, holds out the grim prospect that human societies will finally come to resemble the life of bees, termites, and ants. A perfectly ordered society will exist from generation to generation without change. Everything has been reduced to routine. There is no room to improve anything.[12]

A homely example from my rural Georgia childhood provides a parable of the way pessimists like Ellul, Seidenberg, and Mumford see the modern world. One winter day when I was eleven or twelve years old, I came home from school to find the house cold and empty. My parents were not at home. I built a fire in the fireplace. The wood was dry and soon tall flames leaped up the chimney. It was an old house, and I had been warned against a big fire. In my panic I began to pile on more wood to cover up the cracks through which the flames rose. My solution worked—temporarily. But then an even larger fire developed. I put on still more wood. Each time I smothered the flames for a moment. Finally, I caught on to what was happening. Soon the flames died down, and all was well. The technological pessimists claim that modern humanity is as foolish as I was. As technological reason creates more and more networks of machines and organizations dedicated to rational efficiency, problems are more or less solved—temporarily. But dedication to the technological principle requires more technology to solve problems caused by previous solutions. Meanwhile, the flames grow higher and higher. So far, modern humanity has not caught on and continues to add more technology. Ellul thinks that we are fanatically committed to the use of technological reason to solve our problems. Hence we will probably continue to create networks of control in the name of efficiency and order until we burn our house down. Few have so far seen that the only solution is the rejection of the totalitarianism of technological reason itself.

The optimists employ a symbol which leads to a different vision of the future. For this school of thought, it is the hammer, not the clock, that tells us what technology is and can do for us. Technology is a tool that extends human powers. It solves a problem. The hammer extends the power of the hand. The microscope and the telescope give added refinement to sight. The car, the airplane, and the rocket ship provide a range of mobility that the legs cannot match. The telephone and the radio enlarge the power of the voice to communicate. Technological reason can also solve all sorts of other problems. We can learn how to increase production of food and manufactured goods. We can conquer disease. We can put imagination to work on social problems. We can reduce conflict among people. In short, beginning with the notion that "knowledge is power," we can find ways to meet needs, satisfy wants, and promote happiness. The extension of the hammer principle leads to a future in which knowledge has increased to the point that better ways to do almost everything can be found. The optimists foresee that with the new technology people will make advances in managing their affairs as astonishing as they have made in transforming the physical world. With these tools, they assert, we can begin to shape the world and the conditions of life to fit the heart's desire.

Both the pessimists and the optimists take some selected trends and principles and exaggerate them. Moveover, they do not take into account enough opposing trends and principles.

Using as a basis only one symbol, they make a possible outcome into a probable destiny. But in fact *both* symbols—hammer and clock—point to the nature and consequences of technology. Human powers are extended. Problems can be solved. Means can be found to attain ends. But technological reason functions in one particular way. It is inevitably drawn toward solutions which maximize efficiency, i.e., which allow the greatest amount of production, or service, with the smallest expense of energy and time. Machines and social systems that function like clockwork tend to be the ideal of technological reason. As technological reason is applied to more areas of human life, trade-offs inevitably have to be made. New freedoms are gained at the expense of losing some old ones. To take a simple example, people gain the freedom to travel a two-lane road only by giving up one of the lanes—they must always drive on the right side. This is a rational solution. It enables everybody to get a significant gain at an insignificant cost. Likewise, other extensions of human powers have a price. The hammer, the wheel, the heavy plow, the microscope, and so on, all offer potential benefits which outweigh the costs.

At the early stages it would appear possible, in principle, to use technological reason advantageously with acceptable risks or loss. Optimists claim that a favorable trade-off ratio can be maintained at every stage of advancement if we are prudent. We have, they say, no alternative if we wish to feed, clothe, and house the world's growing population. Pessimists maintain that, after a certain point, the necessities of integrating the whole network of machine and social systems will box in and choke off human freedom. What is clear is that as society becomes more highly organized, the trade-offs get more complicated. The stakes in the game get higher. The perils rise with the opportunities.

It is necessary to challenge the tendency of the pessimists to set up a sharp dualism between the mechanical and the organic (Mumford) or technique and the spiritual (Ellul). Mumford expresses a kind of horror at the sight of an astronaut in a space suit. He sees in it the prototype of a kind of robot existence. Eventually, he says, if the principles of technological reason are taken to their conclusion, life will be "made to conform, as in a space capsule, to the minimal functional requirements of an equally minimal environment—all under remote control."[13] Ellul insists that respect for human responsibility, dignity, and freedom forbids ever acting upon people with technical means. He would agree with the theme of Stanley Kubrick's film, *A Clockwork Orange*. The very title suggests the conflict between the mechanical and the organic, between a machine and the life principle. In this movie, set in some unspecified future, the central character is a young man given to rape, violence, and all sorts of destructive behavior. He also loves Beethoven's music. The authorities capture him and subject him to a process of behavior modification. Chemistry and psychology combine to remake him. When he is released from prison, he grows violently ill at the thought of doing what society forbids. However, he also loses his appreciation for Beethoven. To make a violent man docile by technological means is to destroy his humanity. There is surely a point here that must be heeded.

Nevertheless, those who view technology as a way of enhancing the organic and spiritual capacities of people make an equally compelling case. The hammer does extend the power of the hand. Examples might be multiplied indefinitely, but the point is obvious. Techniques may aid organic functioning. Electronic pacemakers can help a human heart beat normally. Surgical techniques can restore a diseased body to health. Social technologies can contribute to the healthy functioning of a complex modern society. We need better ways of managing the economy, administering welfare, providing health care, and so on. Technologies can be seen as a part of the evolutionary process. They enhance our native powers and extend the range of human adaptability. People have gone beyond their skins in the relationship to the world. "The real evolutionary unit now is not man's mere body; it is 'all mankind's - brains - together - with - all - the - extra - bodily-materials - that - come - under - the - manipulation - of - their-hands.' . . . An airplane is part of a larger kinaesthetic and functional self."[14] This evolutionary, organic enhancement theory of technology is all the more cogent in a day when electronic and cybernetic machines are coming into prominence. The sharp dualism between the natural, the vital, the organic, and the spiritual, on the one hand, and the artificial, the rational, the mechanistic, and the material, on the other, needs to be challenged. We need a more comprehensive view, which takes into account the positive connections between these realms as well as the negative.

The relationship between technology and values is more complex than either the pessimists or the optimists usually allow. Techniques can limit, constrain, mechanize, standardize, and robotize people. Ellul and Mumford see something profoundly threatening and subtle in our growing reliance upon technological reason. But Fuller and Seaborg also see the enhancement of life possible in new technologies: they can feed, clothe, house, cure diseases, remove the burden of poverty, and open new ventures for the human spirit. And all of these people see something that is really there. None of the grand theories that single out particular themes and expand them into the whole truth is adequate. A patient, hardheaded, critical approach is needed, sensitive to the complexities of the social setting in which technology and values interact.

Society is a complex system of relationships in which a multitude of factors influence one another. The causal arrows run in many directions. There are feedback loops which cause ripples of change in complicated ways. Technology produces many of the changes in society, but the effect of those changes depends on many things other than technology itself. As Lynn White says, a new invention opens a door. It does not compel us to enter.[15] Some inventions may lie dormant for a long time before being put to use.

In our own time the disproportionate allocation of funds for the arms race and to send astronauts to the moon was not the result of some inevitable development of technological advance. We could have spent the same amounts for mass housing or urban transportation, if we had so chosen. Technology expresses our values. Furthermore, the impact of technological change depends on how we respond to it. If automation puts people out of work, a number of possibilities arise. The logic of economic power and profits can work to the advantage of corporation owners and to the detriment of employees. The government can intervene to provide income and retraining for displaced workers. The total social context inhibits, promotes, transforms, and otherwise mediates the threats and promises of technological change.

Values affect technology, and technology affects values. In western Europe in the Middle Ages, for example, technology was directly spurred by a belief, namely that there are some kinds of work too degrading for creatures made in the image of God to do.[16] The result of this view was a great increase in the invention of laborsaving devices. In the fifteenth and sixteenth centuries, China had the full capability to explore the world, but chose to stay home. Spain and Portugal decided on a policy of expansion and colonization. Which comes first, the values held by people that lead to inventions or inventions that lead to a change of values? Did the availability of contraceptives lead to change of attitudes toward sexual relations among the unmarried? Or did a change in attitude give impetus to their availability? It is a hen and egg question.[17]

Beyond this, some specific points can be advanced.[18]

1. There is confusion in the claims about what technology can or cannot do. Jerome Wiesner and H. F. York claim that there is no "technical solution" to the dilemma of increasing military power and decreasing national security. They mean that no conceivable increase in weapons superiority can guarantee protection against destruction in a nuclear age. The solution, if there is to be one, must be political. Nations will have to forgo any resort to atomic weapons as a means of combat. In this case, no prospective technology offers a solution either in principle or in fact.[19] Garrett Hardin claims that population and pollution are also in the class of "no technical solution problems." He means that technological advances cannot in themselves provide enough food, reduce the number of births sufficiently, or prevent ecological disaster. There must be a prior change of values that can then be enforced politically.[20] Advanced technologies may offer hope for survival *in principle* but can do so *in fact* only if certain changes in

morality and political behavior take place as well. Buckminster Fuller confidently asserts that engineering science can create the means to provide material plenty and a safe environment for all. His assumption is that only ignorance, inertia, and obsolete ideas stand in the way. In principle, then, technology can solve our basic material problems. But it can do so in fact only if competent planners are granted free reign to solve them. Claims about what technology can and cannot do can easily mislead us unless we are clear about the precise meaning intended.

It is widely accepted, for example, that world population growth has been speeded up by progress in medical practices. New life-saving measures have greatly expanded "death control," but there has been no corresponding increase in "birth control." Technological means are *available* to halt the excessive population rise. But these contraceptive measures are not being used, and the reasons are political, economic, religious, and cultural. They have little relationship to what technology as such can or cannot do. People desire health and long life. Hence, they readily accept modern medical techniques and are willing to pay dearly for them. But people also love children and produce them for many reasons other than sexual pleasure. Thus, they may be reluctant to use contraceptive methods even when they are available. They may find contraception too expensive. Or their religion may teach them that birth control is wrong. Or the ignorance of the population may work against successful use of contraceptives even when people desire to stop having children. Or governments, for a variety of political reasons, may prohibit or discourage birth control. In principle, then, technological reason may be able to provide cures for many of our ills, while in fact, these solutions may not be enacted due to the failure or inability or unwillingness of society to accept the remedy.

Moreover, the problem-solving capacity of technology may not be able to save us from some catastrophes. For example, changes in the climate caused by waste heat released into the atmosphere could lead to global disaster. Weapons exist now that can literally wipe out all life, human and other. These may be unlikely occurrences. Nevertheless, it is quite possible for some technologies to be the source of incurable ills.

2. There is an obvious ambiguity in the uses to which technology can be put. Hence, there is truth—a limited truth—to the claim that technology in itself is neither good nor bad. Certainly a knife can be used to peel apples or to commit murder. Nuclear energy may be used to make bombs or to generate electricity. Viewed in this way, technology needs only to be properly managed in order to maximize its benefits and minimize its dangers. This is the conventional view of the relationship of technology to human values.

But the task of mobilizing our problem-solving powers in ways that promote the good and avoid the evil is horrifyingly complex. Part of the problem is ignorance. Harvey Brooks, an expert in this field, suggests that we are like an untrained person suddenly put into the cockpit of a jet. Before us are complicated sets of dials and levers. The problem is that we don't know how to use them to guide the aircraft safely to our desired destination. At the moment, then, our desire to solve problems exceeds our ability to do so. Many of the current cries for the "taming of technology" are as naive as were the early pleas for planning in the national economy.[21]

But ignorance may be among the less important of our problems. More fundamental are problems which human beings have always faced when trying to shape their future—only now these problems bode incalculable harm because of the growth in population, and the growth in power of technology. Not only ignorance, but greed, anxiety, and the will to power and glory complicate people's desire to be in control of things. We can illustrate this by a quick look at problems that arise both in public and private areas.

Billions upon billions of public dollars have gone into the production of nuclear weapons. We have been afraid not to plunge ahead out of fear of the Russians and the Chinese. But we have been equally fearful that we and our enemies would destroy each other with the very instruments that were designed to protect us. Hence, the arms race takes on a kind of demonic quality. It confronts us as a powerful threat over which we as ordinary citizens have little or no control. A whole generation has grown up under the threat of "the Bomb." The Bomb is the symbol of the terror latent in technology when technology serves human madness (such as the Cold War). The danger of nuclear annihilation has been felt during the last quarter of a century as a kind of Fate. Fate is the very opposite of control. Meanwhile, crying needs around the world go unmet while we waste precious resources in the pursuit of more effective ways to kill people. The arms race represents a complex interweaving of human anxiety and nationalistic idolatry. We have begun to take only the smallest steps toward bringing the idiocy of nuclear escalation to a halt. Those who talk glibly about our ability to take charge of history, should ponder well the technological terror of the arms race.

The space program raises a different set of questions regarding the good use of technology. The billions spent in the effort to put an American on the moon presumably were spent for reasons of national prestige and glory. The effort admittedly was a grand human adventure. However, in light of the pressing needs on earth the question of whether the massive expenditures to explore outer space are morally and socially justifiable is certainly debatable. We keep hearing of the beneficial "spin-offs" the program has generated. Humanity will be benefitted by medical discoveries made in the space effort, we are told. Yet we still wonder if more human welfare could not have been achieved by a different deployment of time, technology, and talent.

The major producers of technological innovations, besides government, are private corporations, whose motives are profit and growth. Our *laissez-faire* policies in this area have tended to produce a chaotic sprawl. The result is a multiplication of technologies that serve corporate profits well, private wants haphazardly, and social needs scarcely at all. Build-in factors in the private enterprise system create an imbalance. It is biased in favor of "economic activities heavy in 'technological content' (for example, new science-based consumer products ... [and opposed to] activities requiring sophisticated social organization (for example, stimulating the economy of the urban ghetto)."[22] As long as our greatest needs were for food, clothing, and other such essentials, the system worked with marginal efficiency. General living standards have risen steadily, but there have always been, and still are great inequities of wealth and income. However, now that more of our needs are public and social (problems of pollution, population, mass transportation, etc.), we need better ways to deal successfully with them. Hence, the use of technology for good purposes runs into three tough problems at once: (1) balancing private wants and social needs; (2) harmonizing the plans made by individual experts with the decisions of the public as a whole; and (3) devising long-range policies in a political system which responds best to immediately felt needs, fears, and wants and which has a generally ill-informed electorate.

3. Technological advances have paradoxical results. This further complicates the social decisions that have to be made. C. F. von Weizsäcker speaks of "ambivalence." Ambivalence occurs when we achieve something other than what was intended even though we do get what was sought.[23] Subduing nature and subjecting it to our wills has led to destruction of the environment. Saving lives through technological progress has helped ignite a population bomb that now threatens many more than were saved. Nuclear weapons, unleashed to shorten a war, now threaten us all with annihilation, and, even when unused, waste billions of dollars in resources. (It is rather desperate comfort to realize that the arms stalemate may in fact be the only reason there is peace—unsteady peace—between Russia and the United States. This is much as if two rich and competing robbers both got terminal cancer and thanked the stars because at least now they couldn't be robbed by each other.) Technology, then, solves some problems, but frequently it creates others that may be even more difficult to solve.

Further, a given change sends out ripples that ultimately affect areas of life far removed from the original situation. Lewis Mumford points out that the invention of the steam engine in the nineteenth century brought enormous benefits. It produced more power, an increase in consumer goods, better transportation, and so on. But other consequences were deplorable. The steam engine led to oppression for miners and other workers, the spread of vast urban slums, and a ruthless stranglehold by capitalistic investors on the wage earner.[24] In the twentieth century, the effects of the automobile have been similarly far-reaching and ambivalent. Transportation has been revolutionized. A new status symbol has emerged. Dating and courtship have been changed. The automobile has even set the pattern of urban development and housing. Today one out of every eight people employed in the United States works at a job directly related to the automobile (supply, maintenance, sales, manufacture, and so on). Some results of the automobile are obviously pernicious, such as highway deaths; but it remains to be seen whether the automobile's destruction of fossil fuels and its creation of pollutants turn out to be even worse problems.

Only a few examples can be given to illustrate the complex interweaving of consequences generated by new technologies.[25] World War II was the first war in which there were more deaths from battle than from disease. The difference was made by widespread use of DDT, invented early in the war. Probably half a billion people are alive now who would be dead except for the use of DDT to eradicate malaria, typhus, and other epidemic scourges in the poorer countries. But today we are terrified by the unforeseen ecological consequences of DDT; it permeates the food chain of plants, insects, animals, and people. Even worse, DDT has greatly contributed to the population explosion, with the result that millions face a future of hunger. If they survive to adulthood, they will confront almost certain unemployment and at best a marginal existence. Widespread starvation has been temporarily delayed by the "Green Revolution"—the introduction of miracle grains that multiply yields several times over. Yet these new grains may be vulnerable to unsuspected diseases that could wipe out whole crops. This could bring disaster to millions who were alive in the first place because of the new varieties. Moreover, the new seeds can be used best by prosperous farmers who have the irrigation and fertilizer needed. The result is another boost for the rich, another blow for the poor. We can see that the effects of technologies spiral upward to create enlarging networks of potential consequences for good or ill.

Medical advances present a whole host of dilemmas. How far shall we go in pursuing measures that keep the hopelessly ill alive? The maintenance of one seriously ill old person may deny resources to many who are less acutely ill but too poor to afford treatment. One can imagine a situation in which we might devote the whole GNP to life-saving procedures. This may happen if we take the logic of keeping people alive to its ultimate conclusion. But how do you decide where the stopping point should be in the light of possible trade-offs? Our technological capacity to save or to prolong life has outrun our economic abilities. Choices are inevitable. With new advances in genetics and medical techniques it is possible to determine many chromosomal defects in embryo. This introduces the possibility of aborting the fetus when great suffering for the individual and great sorrow and cost for the family can be anticipated. Better and better predictions can be made as birth approaches. The optimum time of decision might be in late pregnancy or even after the birth of the child. When and how do you draw the line between abortion and infanticide?

Other baffling problems arise in relation to health and environmental hazards. In the testimony that helped to defeat government support of the supersonic transport plane (SST) in the Senate was a sophisticated item of scientific knowledge. Some experts predicted that the depletion of ozone in the stratosphere due to the exhausts from the SST would produce about 10,000 additional cases of skin cancer in the world. This consequence would follow from the increase in ultraviolet radiation allowed to penetrate through the upper atmosphere. This prediction rested on a complicated theoretical model. Had it not existed, hundreds of supersonic transports might have flown for years before the public noticed the increase in skin cancer. And even then, so many variables are thought to contribute to cancer that the planes might be entirely overlooked as a partial cause.

The effects of air pollution and of the discharge of small amounts of toxic chemicals into the environment are difficult to assess. But increasing knowledge will make it possible to make such measurements more accurately. People are developing lung cancer today because they were exposed to asbestos particles in and around shipyards during World War II.[26] Technology creates environmental dangers, and knowing about these dangers confronts us with problems; we must make choices that did not exist before. And as we do increasingly more powerful things to the environment, the difficulties of resolving these value conflicts will be multiplied. The issue becomes more subtle when it is recognized that the addition of toxic substances to human surroundings does more harm to some groups than to others. The very young, the very old, pregnant women, and those with cardiovascular disease are hurt most. How do we measure this damage done to a few against a social good that may be achieved for many?

Further, decisions made today may create problems or obligations for generations to come. Consider, for example, the storage of radioactive wastes from atomic generating plants. These highly dangerous materials must be kept away from the biosphere for periods of thousands of years with a high degree of reliability. They must be constantly monitored. The storage area must be so impenetrably sealed that no one can ever blunder in. But considering just the political and social cataclysms of this century, can we presume to guarantee such storage sites for even a few years, to say nothing of millennia? Can we obligate posterity to such a danger? Yet producers of electricity claim that there is no way to provide the energy needs of the future without building more atomic reactors that generate dangerous wastes.

Another problem we face from the interweaving of technological advance and human values has been called the "infinitely dangerous, negligible probability accident." Numerous safeguards surround the operation of nuclear reactors. The safety record so far is very good. However, the fact that no serious accident has yet occurred is offset by the massiveness of the catastrophe that would result if the safeguards failed. Hundreds of thousands of people would be killed. Huge areas would be uninhabitable for a long period. How do you weigh values when a danger approaches infinity but the probability of its occurrence approaches zero? In these last examples both progress and safety depend on a highly trained, disciplined elite dealing with issues that have enormous import for the whole society. The most striking instance is the small group of military men who control nuclear weapons. Think especially of the crews of the American and Russian submarines of the Polaris type. Again, there are numerous safeguards, all designed and carried out in secret. Yet our very survival is in their hands. We confront a paradox of the highest order. The routine functions of these people are boring, lonely, and casual. Yet their emergency responsibilities are awesome, requiring unerring judgment and a high level of group trust.

Enough has been said to remind us of the usefulness of the advice given by Alfred North Whitehead: Seek simplicity and distrust it. Harvey Brooks suggests that living with technology is like climbing a mountain which narrows to a knife-edge as the top is reached.[27] Each step takes us higher, but the precipices on either side become steeper. The valley floor below recedes in the distance. The dangers of a misstep increase with each advance. We cannot stop or retreat. We are committed to the peak. The threats we face rise in direct proportion to the promises, and both are climbing at an exponential rate.

The next chapter will develop the concept of visionary reason as the saving counterpart to technological reason. Technological reason serves us best when it becomes the servant of creative thinking and is directed toward life-fulfilling goals. Unless technological reason is dominated by a vision that comes from beyond itself, it will lead us toward robotic efficiency, void of human ecstasy.

CHAPTER 4

Living Between Efficiency and Ecstasy

Technological reason and visionary reason may sound remote from everyday life. They have the ring of abstraction. They suggest the atmosphere of the college classroom. Nevertheless, these terms refer to down-to-earth realities that are shaping the world of today and tomorrow. The way technological reason and visionary reason interact with each other will in large measure decide whether the future should be welcomed or dreaded. Technological reason, by its sheer power, affects our individual destinies every day in many ways. On the other hand, visionary reason, with its goals and values, guides our entire life. Meeting the challenges that lie ahead requires them both. Just what do these terms mean in relationship to each other? Why is it important that technological reason be the servant of visionary reason? The answers to these questions will connect what is going on in the world today with the moral vision rooted in Christian faith.

Technological reason attempts to find the most effective way to achieve a certain goal or solve a given problem. Computers, interstate highways, systems analysis, and intercontinental ballistic missiles are all products of technological reason. So are the miracle wheat and rice of the Green Revolution, the technology of behavior modification proposed by B. F. Skinner,[1] and the computerized model of the global ecology produced by the authors of *The Limits to Growth*.[2] This kind of reasoning operates within the limits of what is possible as defined by (1) the available material and human resources, (2) the laws of nature, and (3) the state of knowledge at the time. It also works within another set of limits that I call boundary conditions. The boundary conditions are set by the persons in charge who make the decisions about the problem that is to be solved. Boundary conditions include (1) a definition of the system or organization that is to be taken into account, (2) the time limits that are to be observed, and (3) the goals to be reached and the means allowable to reach them. Within this framework technological reason aims at getting the job done in the most efficient way, getting the most in its results from the least in its resources.

The problem is that technological reason limits itself to *practical* effectiveness. It is surrounded by larger and deeper value questions that it cannot resolve by itself.[3] The technical expert may make judgments about these more comprehensive issues of good and bad. In order to do this, however, he or she must dip into the reservoir of moral beliefs held as a person. To say it differently, technological reason is an excellent judge of *means* but a poor judge of *ends*. What does it mean to say that technological reason needs the help of visionary reason in deciding what is better or worse for human beings?

It is in the nature of technological reason to maximize results and minimize costs.[4] The decision-makers who are in charge of a given organization or task may specify boundary conditions which forbid certain means. They may demand the inclusion of functions which qualify efficiency. Left to itself, however, technological reason gravitates toward solutions which get the most done with the least expenditure of money, time, or effort. Technological reason is most effective when the information it uses to accomplish its task can be put into mathematical equations. It deals best with what can be weighed, counted, or measured in some way. Technological reason thrives on numbers that can be related to other numbers by a formula. It is better at telling us how to build a bridge than at giving us a cure for a psychotic in a mental hospital. Some human problems confront us in which efficiency is not the most important consideration. Some decisions vital to our welfare do not involve much that we can touch, count, and measure. In these areas it is not easy to get a set of numbers to work with. These are the reasons why there is a tension between the practical effectiveness of technological reason and its total human adequacy. By human adequacy I mean its capacity for dealing with the larger questions of right and wrong, good and bad, which people face in their quest for a satisfying, happy life. This is why visionary reason needs to come into the picture: it deals with these fundamental issues of what the truly good life is and how it is to be achieved humanely.

Imagine the president of a large chain of short-order restaurants who calls in a team of experts to advise him on a human relations problem he is having with his employees.[5] The cooks and the waitresses are fighting. All four of the experts submit a different analysis but all suggest the same solution. (1) The sociologist notes that conflicts occur during rush hours and are related to status problems. Waitresses, lower in status, are required to give orders to the cooks. The solution is a spindle put on the order counter. The waitresses could relay information through this impersonal device and avoid the conflict. (2) The psychologist gives a Freudian interpretation. The manager is the father, the waitress is the daughter, and the cook is the son. When the daughter gives orders to the son, ego problems arise. The remedy is a spindle. (3) The anthropologist sees the issue in terms of a value conflict and proposes a spindle. (4) The systems analyst views the restaurant as an organization that transfers information from one form to another. At times there is a problem of information overload which blocks the flow and threatens to jam the whole system. His cure is a spindle.

Assuming that the spindle solves the problem, the only merit in the interpretations of the first three experts is that they possibly throw some light on the motivations involved. They offer nothing different or better in the way of an answer. Suppose we look further at the work of the systems analyst. By doing so we can get a better idea of how technological reason goes about its job. It takes from the personal relationships among the employees only the information it needs. To put it differently, it abstracts from the total situation only those functions which are relevant to the operation of the system under consideration. The whole person Joe is reduced to his "cook function." Mary is seen in terms of her "waitress function."

Other people serve a "customer function," "manager function," and so on. It is easy to see how thinking of the problem in this way aids one in deciding how the job can be done with the least cost and energy. We can also see what the pessimists mean when they argue that technological reason in its quest for rational efficiency tends to reduce people to a cog in the social machine. When technological reason has organized all human activities and found absolutely the most efficient way to do everything, then people will indeed have become things. So the pessimists claim.

To pursue our example further, suppose now the systems analyst enlarges his task and inquires whether the functions of the waitresses and cooks could be fully automated. Costs could be reduced by installing a device for ordering and delivering food to customers at their tables. Automation would be indicated, unless customers would rather pay more for food served by waitresses. Suppose it does turn out to be more profitable to automate the restaurant and fire the waitresses. At this point the president of the chain faces a decision: how will he draw the boundary conditions? He might decide to take into account the larger communities in which the restaurants are located. Conceivably he might conclude that the damage done through an increase in unemployment outweighs the value of his private gain. But obviously, some powerful motives operate in favor of firing the people and installing machinery. Three come to mind at once: (1) the company's immediate self-interest, (2) the logic of free enterprise capitalism, and (3) the bias of technological reason towards efficiency. Nevertheless, the systems analyst cannot do his job until the president of the food chain has weighed these considerations and decided. Will the president view the restaurant as simply a profit-making enterprise? Will he see his business as a responsible member of a larger community whose welfare must also be considered? How will he decide between his immediate private gain and the increase in unemployment that automation would cause?

At this point a slippery but very important problem arises. Technological reason always seeks immediately a better way to do something. Ultimately, it looks for the one best possible way that can be found. However, confusion may arise over what constitutes the definition of better. The logic of technological reason says that better means more efficient. But better is also determined by what the people making the decisions want. Automating the restaurant may be more efficient. Yet the president of the food chain may decide against automation because it would cause a loss of jobs for his employees. Here is where a good deal of discussion gets bogged down. People holding contrary points of view talk right past each other. Pessimists fear that solving problems by technological reason means that efficiency will finally prevail everywhere. Optimists claim that technological reason takes orders from whoever is in charge: they will decide what goals are to be sought and who is to benefit, and so ultimately everything depends on their values. Technological reason just seeks for the best way to do what people want done. Both the pessimists and the optimists are right in what they include. They are misleading or incomplete in what they leave out.

Is technological reason itself empty of any values other than efficiency? Is it simply the slave of orders that come from somewhere else? Has it no word of its own to offer about the larger questions of human welfare?

1. Technological reason does not so much ignore human welfare as come at it indirectly. A well-tuned motor saves money for the car owner. It also reduces pollution and eases the drain on dwindling fuel supplies. Hence, people benefit when efficiency is increased. In the example of the restaurants, automation would produce greater profits. If reinvested in the communities, such profits could lead to greater total employment and a rise in general prosperity for everybody. Efficiency makes it possible for people to get more of what they want with the resources they have.

2. Technological reason is led by its own logic to enlarge the perspective within which it works. This enlargement includes a shift from short-term to long-term considerations. In order for a smaller unit to survive, the larger unit which contains it will have to be preserved. No matter how efficient the liver is, it cannot function at all if the body to which it belongs dies. On

this basis, technological reason can argue against continuing the rapid growth of population, pollution, industrial production, and use of natural resources. If growth is not curbed, the result will be eventual collapse of the global ecological system.

A value system is implicit in technological reason. Its ultimate point of reference is the viability of the largest unit that must be finally taken into account. What are the largest sets of requirements that must be met in order to keep any given system going for a long period of time? Survival becomes the final appeal. Insofar as there is an identity or connection between survival and human welfare, we are dealing with a valid moral principle. Hence, technological reason can help specify the minimal requirements of keeping something alive and functioning. However, if human beings desire not only to live but to live well and to live better, then technological reason alone cannot suffice. An ethical perspective is implicit in this form of problem solving, but it is minimal and incomplete.

Suppose that a problem arises in a large industrial plant. Study shows the facts to be as follows: (1) The productivity of black employees is substandard due to low morale as the consequence of continued discrimination. (2) White workers will not tolerate any change that might threaten their advantages.[6] The problem is to increase productivity among the blacks without causing unmanageable turmoil among the whites. Further research indicates that it would be possible to get the desired results in two different ways. (1) One method would be to use propaganda techniques, along with some minor compensations to blacks. Morale would be boosted, but the basic discriminations would remain. (2) The other plan would involve mild coercion and moral suasion to reduce white resistance to racial equality.

The principle of efficiency alone gives no basis for choosing between these alternatives. The managers might decide for the second if they believed in racial justice. They might choose the first if they were prejudiced. Those who have the power of making decisions (determining boundary conditions) in situations like this are powerful indeed. In this situation the personal values of the decision-makers make all the difference.

However, technological reason itself might decide on its own principles. The argument would be that in the long run the company would flourish best in a society that had achieved equality between the races. Hence, it would be better to eliminate white prejudice than to smooth over black discontent. But note that this approach to social justice is indirect and pragmatic. In the case we are considering, the most efficient way to run the company just *happened* to be the most moral. It does not always work out that way.

To summarize, technological reason can operate within two different settings. (1) It may function under strict orders from somewhere else. These orders (boundary conditions) lay down in detail the goals to be sought and the means to be used to achieve them. (2) It may proceed on its own, using its own logic. This logic specifies that efficiency within an assigned system may depend on the health of some larger system to which it is connected. The principle involved is similar to what we call "enlightened self-interest." In most cases, these two ways of operating will intersect and overlap. Pessimists like Ellul are worried that in the modern world the second is rapidly taking over. The first way is being squeezed out. Our use of technological reason is gradually causing us to link all networks and systems involving both machines and people. This linkage is necessary to keep them operating in harmony with each other. And gradually, the demands of "the system" are becoming more difficult to avoid or resist. The eventual consequence is that we will come to serve "the system" rather than having it serve us. Ellul's horror, this slavery to our systems, is one of the futures open to us, but not the only one. It all depends on whether visionary reason can keep the logical tendencies of technological reason under control. Just what is visionary reason? How does it work?

Reason is the gift we have from God that enables us to gain understanding of the world. It also helps us find our way toward a good and satisfying life. Reason, then, has two sides: (1) it provides understanding and (2) it guides action. Hence, we speak of theoretical reason and of practical reason. We commonly distinguish between theory and practice, yet we should not separate them too sharply. Science and philosophy are basically forms of theoretical reason. Yet they have practical implications for life. Technology and theology are basically forms of practical reason. Yet each has a theoretical side.[7] Visionary reason is practical in nature. It is the steering agency that enables people to cope with, adapt to, and act upon their environment. All this is done in quest of the best satisfactions life can offer. Visionary reason aims not only at the good but at the better and the best.

In the words of Alfred North Whitehead, theoretical reason is the disinterested search for complete understanding which Plato shares with the gods. Practical reason is the effort to devise an immediate course of action which Ulysses shares with the foxes.[8] By this definition, reason is not unique to people. It is found in some form throughout nature. We can gain new appreciation for the unity of all living things if we recognize that what we know as reason in humanity has its counterpart at a lower level in the animal world. Birds build nests. People build houses. Beavers build dams with logs. People build them with concrete. The higher animals pursue their food. Human beings domesticate cattle. Insects have evolved a complex social organization with elaborate divisions of labor. The relatives of Plato and Ulysses form governments and invent the assembly line. Chimps use a chopstick to dig eggs out of an anthill. Termites have air-conditioned dwellings. Bats have radar. Dolphins have sonar. People invent tools. Reason in humanity unites Plato with the gods while at the same time uniting Ulysses with the foxes.

The visionary reason of God is at work in the whole process of nature. This accounts for the first appearance of life on earth. It explains the emergence of successively higher species over long billions of years. This drama has culminated in the appearance of human beings. In humanity reason takes a unique form. We have the intelligence and the imagination to begin to understand what has happened in the past and led up to the present. We can also use our imagination to invent a better future. People are dreamers who can envision states yet unrealized. People are doers who can build a road toward utopia.

Reason "directs and criticizes the urge towards the attainment of an end realized in imagination but not in fact."[9] The Bible teaches that humanity was made in the image of God. Guided by intelligence and imagination, the human search for the good life is a reflection of the visionary reason of God. God's visionary reason guides the whole universe and all of history toward his goal—namely, the Kingdom of heaven about which the Bible speaks.

The task of reason is to promote the art of life, Whitehead says, and he goes on to offer us a memorable phrase. Reason, he declares, acts in obedience to a threefold urge: "to live, . . . to live well, . . . and to live better."[10] Survival is the first aim of living beings, but not the last. Life comes with a built-in desire to experience to the fullest all the pleasures and joys of being alive. Not only that, it also comes with a drive to go beyond any present state of achievement in quest of what is better. A theologian who lived 1500 years before Whitehead expressed similar thoughts in these remarkable lines:

> Truly the very fact of existing is by some natural spell so pleasant, that even the wretched are, for no other reason, unwilling to perish; and, when they feel that they are wretched, wish not that they themselves be annihilated, but that their misery be . . . [removed]. . . . is it not obvious . . . how nature shrinks from annihilation? . . . What! Do not even all irrational animals, . . . from the huge dragons down to the least worms, all testify that they wish to exist, and therefore shun death by every movement in their power? Nay, the very plants and shrubs, . . . do not they all seek, in their own fashion, to conserve their existence, by rooting themselves more and more deeply in the earth, so that they may draw nourishment, and throw out healthy branches towards the sky?[11]

How do we account for the tenacity with which plants, animals, and human beings hang on to life? Why do they strive with all their might to live out their existence in the fullest way possible? St. Augustine suggests the answer. Life is enjoyable. By "some natural spell" existence is so pleasant that even the wretched don't want to die. They want their misery removed. People commit suicide because they have lost hope that their wretchedness can be overcome. They would prefer to live, if only their pain and unendurable sorrow could be taken away. Enjoyment, then, is the supreme reason for being and staying alive.[12] When the author of Genesis 1 says that God looked at all that he had made and saw that it was good, very good, what was meant? I think the writer intended to say that it is good *to be*. Enjoyment is experiencing the goodness of being. Existence is inherently valuable, worthwhile. The higher we go up the scale of life from plants to animals to people, the greater capacity there is for enjoying the goodness of being. God, the inspired writer of Genesis tells us, made everything good. The implication is that God experiences the keenest enjoyment of all.

Do plants have feelings? I don't know. Certainly there is a difference between health and disease and between life and death in trees, flowers, weeds, and grass. I can look out my window right now and see a garden filled with beautiful poppies in full bloom. In order for poppy seeds to grow to maturity and produce blossoms and new seeds, they must have the right combination of air, temperature, soil, rain, and sunshine. Health in a flower occurs when conditions are such that the potentiality in the seed is developed. This process leads to the production of colorful petals. The seed "knows" how to become a flower. It has the urge "to live, to live well and to live better." All it needs is the opportunity. It will strive with all its might and "reason" to stay alive and grow. If a pebble is on top of it, it will find a way around, if possible. It will do all it can to get to the sunshine.

Animals and people, of course, are more complicated in their needs and in their capacities for enjoyment. Nevertheless, the general principle holds for them as well as for plants. They are healthy and they enjoy their existence if their potentialities can be brought to flower. If a human being is to grow to full enjoyment, its physical needs must be met from the time it is born. As a child, it needs to grow up in a family surrounded by love. And as an adult, it requires opportunities for developing and expressing its talents and for fulfilling its ambitions. If these conditions are met, the resulting health of body and spirit will be experienced as enjoyment. Enjoyment is the feeling one has inside when the possibility given at birth is being actualized. To live in bodily health, to participate in loving human relationships, and to engage with society in physical, mental, moral, and spiritual adventures, is to bring the whole potential of one's life to full bloom. This is what the creation story means when it tells us of the goodness of all beings. Human life is to be enjoyed. It comes with that built-in possibility and desire. Life is enjoyable when its capacities for good are realized. In considerable measure, of course, we spoil our capacities by actions and choices that are ignorant, foolish, selfish, and destructive. Nevertheless, our "fallenness" and sinfulness do not change the fact that God's intention built into the creation is that life should be enjoyed.

Enjoyment does not refer simply to the pleasures of the body. That is part of it. Many Christians are suspicious of the sensuous side of life. Erskine Caldwell in his novel *God's Little Acre* has the old man Ty Ty say something like this: "Coffee is so good, I don't know why it's not a sin to drink it." But the supreme end of life is not some particular pleasure of the body. Neither is it some specific joy of the spirit. What is enjoyed is *life itself*. I am speaking of the joy in being, in living. It is good *to be*. This kind of enjoyment occurs when the possibilities that come with life are realized in healthy, full, and positive ways. Just as our bodies need food, so our spirits need to love and be loved. Life is enjoyed when the needs of the body and the requirements of the spirit are fulfilled.

Enjoyment, then, refers to the inner experience that accompanies a healthy state of body and spirit. Now and then there are moments when enjoyment reaches an especially intense climax in what the mystics might call the vision of God. In these transient and occasional "mountain top" experiences, the whole self is flooded with an overwhelming sense of being united in love with all of life and with its ultimate source. One day, in the spring of 1955, I was returning to my apartment from a class at Emory University in Atlanta, Georgia. The sky was blue. The sun was shining brightly. The wind was blowing softly through the grove of pine trees through which I was walking. Suddenly, unexpectedly, I was filled with an intense feeling of joy. I had a direct, immediate, unqualified, intuitive awareness of the sheer pleasure of being alive. Somehow it seemed that all of nature around me shared the experience. All around me was the busy world of humanity full of conflict, suffering, and dying. But in that quick moment in the pine trees, I knew deeply that creation was very good. Such fleeting moments of religious ecstasy are enjoyed for their own sake. So are those experiences of loving union with others which now and then exalt our feelings to the point of perfect joy. These occasions represent the attainment of life's highest good. They are a means to nothing at all beyond themselves.

To summarize, practical reason moves between two poles. At the one extreme are the rules of mathematics which guide technological reason in its search for the most efficient way of achieving some limited and prescribed goal. We use that kind of reasoning upon those things, quantities, and relationships which can be manipulated and controlled with the precision of numbers. At the other extreme are those moments of ecstatic joy which are the zenith in our quest for the good life. The reasoning associated with those events can only experience and seek; for nothing that occurs in our ecstatic moments can be manipulated or controlled. This is not to deny that there are spiritual disciplines that can increase our chances of experiencing these mystical moments. It is only to say that this is the realm of grace in which we are surprised by free gifts. We can only receive them with gratitude and hope that the Giver will surprise us again soon.

Most human experience lies somewhere between these absolute limits of efficiency and ecstasy. The daily lot of all of us is caught up in the rhythm and flow of ordinary life with its routine duties. We experience varying mixtures of joy and sorrow, success and failure. This is life in its common ordinariness in which we try at least to preserve our sanity and at most to improve our lot and that of others around us. In these everyday settings what I have called technological reason and visionary reason intersect and overlap. The former focuses on means, the latter on ends. In most everyday experiences, the relationship between these two forms of practical reason is that between problem solving and goal setting. The chimpanzee using a stick to get eggs from an anthill, a child figuring out how to tie her wagon to a tricycle, and the country politician developing a strategy to get elected to the legislature all illustrate the interweaving of imagining ends and inventing means. Likewise, a space team designing Skylab, an economist working on the challenge of inflation in the midst of recession, and a pastor searching for ways to revitalize a congregation show in many forms the interdependence of technological reason and visionary reason. So do a thousand other operations of common reasoning about ordinary things.

In the modern world the technical side of practical reason has taken a more scientific form. It works best with information that can be translated into numbers and put into a formula or equation. Technological reason is thereby limited in perspective, shallow, and incomplete. It obscures both the heights and depths of the larger meanings and purposes of life. Visionary reason is directed toward the more inclusive and ultimately toward ultimate goals. It pulls technological reason upward toward the vision of God and resists the gravitational pull toward an ethical outlook which knows no appeal beyond survival.

Visionary reason is rooted in the evolutionary origin and history of life. It reaches its highest expression in the Christian dream of the Kingdom of God. The Biblical idea of the final end envisions a community of persons united to each other in mutual love and to God in loving adoration. All evil is banished and blessedness reigns without qualification. For Christian believers this is the supreme ideal entertained in imagination but not yet realized in fact. Obviously, the moral principles and social goals implied in this vision do not at present dominate the world. Even Christians seldom rise to the moral heights pictured by this vision. Judged by the ideals of the Kingdom, most forms of visionary reason are deficient in ways that range from ignorance to idolatry. Selfishness, greed, fear, insecurity, pride, prejudice, and hate distort the motives and morality of human beings. "Everybody looks out for number one!" This is the common way of expressing the fact that individuals, groups, and institutions are most strongly motivated to strive for goals that benefit them. Moreover, the unavoidable trade-offs among competing values further prevent the real world of stubborn facts from being more fully transformed into the ideal of Christian imagination.

The task of visionary reason in this situation is to keep pressing the questions about what human life is and what it ought to be. What are human beings good for? What is good for them? For what destiny were we made? What potentialities are given with life? How can they be realized so as to produce the greatest range and depth of enjoyment? What did God intend us to be and to do? What would it mean here and now for us to do the will of God on earth as it is done in heaven? For the Christian, human potentialities and achievements are to be measured in the light of the creating, redeeming love of God manifested in Jesus. Christian visionary reason acts in accordance with the ideals of the Kingdom of God. This is the end for which the Spirit strives. Ideally, the church should be the bearer of Christian visionary reason. It should be the searchlight of humanity which points out the path to the future—an earthly city made in the image of the New Jerusalem. But however grand the ideal is, it must also be made specific and applicable to everyday situations now. The vocation of the Christian is to keep one eye on the future city made perfect. The other eye should be on the immediate decisions and situations faced day by day in our present, still-imperfect city. In factories, schools, offices, laboratories, and government, Christians have many opportunities to draw boundary conditions. Their aim should be to create and enlarge the possibilities of human fulfillment, as marked out by the path that leads to the future God wills. Without a vision of the ideal future as our goal, we do not even know what direction to start in. Without a road map that tells how to get there from here, the goal can never be reached. *To dream and to do, to imagine and to invent, to will and to work, to envision the distant goal and to institute a present plan*—these are the inseparable twins that define the role of visionary reason.

Between the ultimate and the immediate, there are many intermediate stages having to do with everyday, ordinary life. The goals of visionary reason can be worked out in detail only by those who know the facts of every particular situation. The plan of attack in every case involves the three dimensions of knowledge, decision making, and goal setting. To be more specific, the cybernetic model claims that the machinery of any self-correcting, goal-directed organization is made up of receivers of information, a control center, and effectors of action. Healthy functioning requires a flow of information back and forth to keep things working correctly. To correct any wrong or to improve any situation, four things are necessary: (1) an analysis of the ailment, complete with detailed facts; (2) communication of this analysis to those who have authority to make changes; (3) persuasion or coercion of those in authority to order some desirable changes; and (4) effective transmittal of orders and effective use of means to carry them out. The effort to change things for the better can break down at any point. This is a simplified summary. Nevertheless, this recipe for correcting or improving an organization applies to the simplest and to the most complex situations.[13]

There are two parts to every criticism of the functioning of an organization: the technical and the moral. The technical side points out that a function is not being carried out properly because of some fault in the machinery. The moral aspect points out that the function itself is defective. The first deals with facts, the real. The second deals with values, the ought. The technical dimension calls for "scientists"—for expert knowledge and technical ability. The moral dimension calls for "saints"—for sensitivity and insight into what hurts and what helps people.[14] These two dimensions correspond to the roles of technological and visionary reason. The former looks for effective means to carry out assigned ends or functions. The latter seeks to insure that the ends are good, right, and life-fulfilling. Both forms of practical reasoning seek what is better.

For technological reason, better means more efficient. For visionary reason, better means more beneficial to people. These concerns intersect and overlap, though they proceed from different motives.

Every reader can make this analysis specific by thinking of an organization that he or she knows well—church, family, school, office, factory, laboratory, government bureau, hospital, or whatever. Each will find that whenever he has evaluated the organization or suggested change, he has combined technical and moral aspects in his thought. There is something of the "scientist" and something of the "saint" in all of us. The church's task is to sensitize us to the ideals and goals needed for the coming Kingdom of God. The church must help us become more "saintly" in our jobs and in our communities. At present, in our vocations and in other parts of our daily lives, most of us are probably making the most use we can of our scientific knowledge and practical technique. Our aim for the future should be to raise the *moral* level of whatever organizations we are in. As Christians we have a binding obligation to make fullest use of our moral insights and creative imaginations to work for what is of most benefit to people. Our question in every situation should be: What would it mean here and now if the will of God were done on earth as it is in heaven? I have no illusions at all that this is an easy or painless task.

The final part of this book is to spell out in some detail the ethics of the Kingdom of God, and to specify what mission the church might undertake as the bearer and nourisher of Christian visionary reason. Can the church help citizens of the emerging postindustrial society be more "saintly" in their "scientific" endeavors? I believe it can.

CHAPTER 5

Living on Earth for Heaven's Sake

THE WILL OF GOD IS TO MAKE HEAVEN REAL. This sentence serves better than most to capture the theme that runs from Genesis to Revelation. God's purpose is to create a loyal people and to bring them to a good future. In this coming Kingdom, the joy of life will be brought to a perfection that is never to be lost again. This idea takes many forms and undergoes a long development. The final goal is progressively enriched in scope and content.[1] In the beginning, Abraham is promised only that all the nations will be blessed through his numerous progeny. In the end John is given a magnificent vision of the New Jerusalem coming down out of heaven, full of radiant splendor. Between Genesis and Revelation the Bible is filled with varying conceptions of the end soon to come, and it is impossible to reconcile all these dreams of the imminent glory. Each reflects the conditions of a given time; each expresses the faith of the community at one stage of its development. Yet through them all, there is one constant theme: the will of God is to make heaven real.

The prophets of the Old Testament provide us with a vantage point for seeing this grand motif in clearer focus. These inspired proclaimers of the Divine Word begin by reminding Israel of her deliverance from Egypt's bondage. They speak of the covenant made at the time of Moses. Their constant message is that God chose those escaped slaves for a special mission and a destiny, but God hinged his offer on the demand that they live in steadfast love and loyalty. The past, however, is not these prophets' primary focus. Expectation, not memory, is their forte. Their fervor is most manifest in their visions of what is still to come for the Lord's chosen. Beyond the catastrophic judgment required to purge Israel's heart and vindicate God's honor, a new day awaits. In this coming age the promise of a perfected Kingdom will be fulfilled.

In the classical period of prophecy running from Amos to II Isaiah (750-550 B.C.), three characteristics of the good future stand out. (1) PEACE. Hostility will end in nature and in history. Harmony will prevail between humankind and beast and between one animal species and another. Swords will be beaten into plowshares, spears into pruning hooks. Nations will learn war no more (Is. 2:4*b*). The wolf will dwell with the lamb. The leopard and the kid will lie down together. A child will lead them around without harm (Is. 11:6-9). (2) RIGHTEOUSNESS. The rebellion of Israel will cease. Love, loyalty, and obedience to God will be perfected. A new covenant will bring intuitive knowledge of God and of the Law to all people (Jer. 31:23-34). The messiah of the house of David will see to it that the poor and the weak get justice. No person or nation will oppress another (Is. 11:1-4). (3) PROSPERITY. The love of the Hebrew for the earth and this bodily life appears repeatedly in the prophetic writings. Health, wealth, and the pleasures of the flesh will fill the heart with delight. No child will die in infancy. All will live to a ripe old age. Fields and vineyards will produce in abundance (Is. 65:17-26). The threshing floors will be heavy with grain. The vats will overflow with wine and oil (Joel 2:24-26). Jerusalem will be a mother with breasts full of milk. Her inhabitants will suck until satisfied, carried upon her hip, and dandled on her knee (Is. 66:12-13). These passages chosen almost at random could be duplicated many times. Freed from external oppression, the chosen people will live in harmony with nature and with each other in a prosperous land. Peace, justice, and joy will reign supreme. A reconciled remnant will fill the air with songs of exalted praise to the Giver of salvation.

The prophets grew ecstatic about the good future that God would bring. Yet they were not dreamers with their heads in the clouds, knowing little and caring less about what went on around them. Invoking what God had done and would do to fulfill the promises to Abraham and Moses, the prophets spoke with startling clarity about the moral corruption around them. Their words make vivid the thunderous judgments of the Holy One of Israel. They are unrelenting in their denunciations of injustice—injustice that cried out on every side like a stench. Pride, haughtiness, lying, cheating, stealing, and all crimes imaginable were rampant; and each crime spelled rebellion against the Creator and Ruler. Ritual and formal ceremony had become the hypocritical substitutes for trustful obedience. Idolatry was everywhere. Wanton lawlessness made a mockery of decent living. Kings sought power and glory by the violent spilling of blood. The people were mired in immoralities and gave vent to every licentious desire of spirit and flesh. The rich and resourceful crushed the rights of the poor and helpless. For these ungrateful covenant-breakers catastrophe lay in store: they forgot the mercy God showed to their forebears, so God would forget his mercy to them. Before any divine promise could be consummated, a terrible "day of the Lord" would have to purge this people. Only a remnant cleansed by the fire would remain to inherit the Kingdom.

In the postexilic period, Israel experienced a deepening sense of evil in history. Under the influence of Persian religion and the unending oppression by foreigners from Assyria to Rome, an otherworldly outlook developed. The conviction grew up that only in another realm beyond the end of this age could the triumph of God take place. This "apocalyptic" view distinguished the present era under the domination of Satan from the age to come. On the last day God would intervene directly in human affairs and overcome Satanic powers. The righteous would be vindicated, and the whole world subjected to the beneficent command of the divine will.

It was within this framework of thought that Jesus appeared. His message was that the long-awaited Kingdom was finally at hand (Mark 1:14-15). In his own words and deeds the new age was already beginning. It would soon be consummated at the appearance of the Son of Man. In the light of the Kingdom's coming, his hearers were urged to repent, believe, and be obedient to the radical moral demands of the Almighty.

For those who wanted to receive the Kingdom, the message was plain: love God with all your being and love your neighbor as yourself.

The message of the New Testament is that the old age under the domination of sin and death is coming to a close. The new age of righteousness and life hovers near ready to break through in all its might and glory. Christ has vanquished the powers of darkness. Reconciliation for sin has been made by his atoning death. His resurrection is the beginning of a victory over death that is to be shared by all the faithful at the endtime. God is beginning to make heaven real; therefore, repent of sin, accept the gift of salvation with gratitude, and show to all the love manifest in Jesus himself. That is the good news that floods the writings of the apostles. As in the prophets, divine action and human ethics are inseparable. Hope based on faith in God's future, and love based on God's own redemptive love —these are the twin motifs of the ethics of the Kingdom.

The Bible proclaims a God-centered religion. It describes a drama that moves from creation to consummation. At the center of the story is a Sovereign Person who strives to bring the world to a perfect end. A Kingdom is to be established that the faithful can enjoy forever. God is pictured as living purposive will. The prophets and apostles set forth the quality and the aim of the mighty acts of God. Within this framework we can grasp the fundamentals of the ethics of the Kingdom. The central principle can be stated as follows: REPRODUCE IN YOUR ACTIONS TOWARD OTHERS THE QUALITY AND AIM OF THE SAVING ACTS OF GOD TOWARD YOU.[2] The *quality* of divine working is defined as that special kind of love shown in the life, deeds, and death of Jesus of Nazareth. The *aim* of the acts of God is to establish the Kingdom.

Whether we look at the Old Covenant or the New, the same pattern appears. The Ten Commandments are preceded by a statement of the divine activity which made them possible:

> And God spoke all these words, saying, "I am the LORD your God, who brought you out of the land of Egypt, out of the house of bondage. You shall have no other gods before me. . ." (Ex. 20:1-3)

And when Jesus comes into Galilee preaching, his message takes a similar form:

> The time is fulfilled, and the kingdom of God is at hand; repent and believe in the gospel. (Mark 1:15)

God's action to bring in the Kingdom is the basis for the call to repentance and faith. Many of the epistles of the New Testament open by declaring that God has acted in the world to save it by coming in the person of Christ. Following this relation of what God has done, and a call to faith, the epistles proceed to outline the ethical requirements which God's new works command. The scheme of the epistles is like this:[3]

gospel message	*ethical teachings*
Romans 1–11	Romans 12–16
Galatians 1–4	Galatians 5
Ephesians 1–3	Ephesians 4–6
Colossians 1–2	Colossians 3–4

The same idea appears when Christ is said to be the example of the way God acts toward us. Hence, we are to reproduce in our actions toward others the pattern of the act of God in Christ.

> Let each of you look not only to his own interests, but also to the interests of others. Have this mind among yourselves, which you have in Christ Jesus, who, though he was in the form of God, did not count equality with God a thing to be grasped, but emptied himself, taking the form of a servant. . . . (Phil. 2:4-7*a*)

Ethics is set within the context of God's action and promise. An announcement is made of a divine deed that creates a different cosmic and historical situation. There follows a call for human response to this new state of affairs. The demonic powers who rule the present age have been dealt a fatal blow by the saving deed of God in Christ. Though only a foretaste of the final victory to come, the new creation is already present. All are called upon now to receive their freedom from sin and death. They are urged to accept their status as mature heirs of the Kingdom and live in grateful obedience to God's demands.

There is a *gospel* of grace: God loves you and accepts you as you are. There is a *law* of love: love your neighbor, even the enemy and the undeserving brother or sister. God showed love by sending Jesus, who loved you and forgave you even when you killed him. Forgive as you have been forgiven. Accept the other person, worthy or not, as God accepted you. The first note of the gospel is that God loves us with the quality of love that is seen in Jesus. The second note is that we should love one another with the same kind of love. The good news is that God's aim is to make heaven real. The ethical demand is that we manifest the reality of heaven on earth by making God's aim our own. In short, there are two ways of stating the Christian moral imperative. (1) Love your neighbor as you love yourself. (2) Let the supreme goal of your action be the coming of the Kingdom of God on earth. Taken together, they express the quality and the aim of God's action, which is to be the model of human response. Each presupposes and leads to the other. The love of neighbor expresses the reality of the Kingdom. The coming to be of the Kingdom requires the love of neighbor.

A contemporary interpretation of the ethics of the Kingdom must be quite clear on two important points.

1. The New Testament teaches that the Kingdom is primarily a gift of God, not a human achievement. It is established by God's activity when, and how, God chooses. Jesus announces the breaking in of the Kingdom as an objective reality which his hearers must take into account. Repentance, faith, and obedience are the prerequisites for sharing in the new age, not strategies for making that age happen. Those who decide for God will inherit the Kingdom and become its citizens. Those who do not will be cast into outer darkness. The coming of the Kingdom in its fullness is to be a sudden, catastrophic, cosmic, and supernatural occurrence.

However, the Kingdom of God is not simply a future reality. It is also a present power that has already broken into history. And in this present form, the Kingdom can be filled out and completed by human acts. Trustful obedience and service of neighbor express publicly and visibly the reality of the new age that has come, is coming, and will come. By reproducing in actions toward others the quality and aim of God's act to them, believers become co-workers with God and co-creators of the Kingdom. The Kingdom, then, comes both by divine and human action. The Kingdom *is* present and *will be* universally triumphant. Let its reality be made manifest in your decisions and deeds. Participate in the coming to be of the Kingdom by making God's aim your own.

2. The expected end did not occur. The prophetic vision of a messianic age of peace, righteousness, and prosperity which was to transform the land of Israel into an everlasting paradise never became a reality. The cosmic cataclysm foreseen by the books of Daniel and Revelation has not rendered the powers of darkness impotent. Sin, death, and moral confusion are still with us. Jesus expected the final day to take place within the lifetime of some of his hearers. Over and over John tells the readers of his Apocalypse that the end will come "soon." Prophets and apostles from Isaiah to 2 Peter have announced that the long-awaited deliverance was finally at hand. None of these predictions came true. God has not yet made heaven real in this ultimate sense. The world goes on. To argue that the end spoken of in either Old or New Testament is still to happen at some near or far off time is to do violence to the plain words of the text.

What we must do is reexamine thoroughly the ideas which the prophets and apostles had about the future. Without this, we can hardly use them as our basis for ethical action in the twentieth century. I intend to connect the Biblical message of a divinely willed good future with the idea of visionary reason. The creative activity of God in nature and in history is prior to human action. Indeed, human action is simply the latest result of God's action in evolving this world.[4] Over vast stretches of time a spectacular adventure has been taking place on earth. From simple matter came life. From life came conscious mind. Evolution is a history of creative advance. New forms of life have emerged, with more complicated nervous systems that increase their ability to act creatively on their environment and to experience enjoyment.

Billions of years after the first self-reproducing molecule

began the chain of life, a peculiarly gifted creature appeared at the top of the evolutionary scale. Human beings were unlike anything ever seen on earth. Possessed of a high-powered brain in an unusually versatile body, they were set apart most radically by their ability to stand back and ask what it all means. This capacity for wonder and imagination is a basic mark of being human. God gave us an insatiable curiosity about the origin, meaning, and destiny of life. What kind of creature is this anyway who can ask such questions? The writers of Genesis claimed that in the creation of Adam and Eve we see beings made in God's own image. Just as God can imagine new possibilities and bring them into being, so can we in a human way. People are dreamers with powers to make dreams begin to come true.

My claim, then is twofold: (1) What appears in human beings as creative imagination can be seen throughout nature in less advanced forms. It is foreshadowed in the ability of all living things to adapt to their surroundings and to increase their chances of surviving and reproducing. (2) The creative imagination of humankind reflects the visionary reason of God—God's will to create a world and direct it toward a final goal of perfection. The basic theme of the Bible is that God works in nature and in human affairs to make heaven real. Many passages of Scripture teach that the universe itself will be included in the achievement of the final goal. Paul writes that "the creation itself will be set free from its bondage to decay and obtain the glorious liberty of the children of God." (Rom. 8:21) The Bible tells the story of inspired prophets and apostles who dreamed a dream of a perfected world that God will at last bring into being. At the human level the divine aim is to establish a community of persons united in love and free from all the ills that spoil the enjoyment of life. This is God's dream and comes to reality by God's action; but it is also God's will that it be our dream, and come to reality in part by our acts. We are made in the image of God—that is, we have visionary reason which is creative, like God's—and our visionary reason gives us the privilege of being co-creators with God in the final goal.

Against this background we can develop further the ethics of the Kingdom. The central principle is that we should reproduce in our own actions the quality and the aim of God's prior actions toward us. The quality (love) and the aim (heaven) of God's action are interdependent. Each presupposes and leads to the other. Love of neighbor expresses the reality of the Kingdom. The coming to be of the Kingdom requires love of neighbor. The two emphases also point out the relationship between present and future in Christian morality. The command to love your neighbor is oriented to here and now. It directs attention to immediate needs. It requires compassion for the suffering and oppressed people in our midst. It compels us to attack the worst evils of the moment. However, in order to meet the needs of our neighbors and relieve their miseries fully, we must look ahead. The quest for the coming Kingdom directs us to create conditions most likely to increase human welfare. And that effort looks toward the future. Loving our neighbors here and now, then, requires that we work toward the fullest welfare of both them and all people, which is the Kingdom. And working for the Kingdom in the future calls for loving our neighbors here and now.

Another word for the Kingdom is heaven; and it too has a twofold reference. (1) Heaven is a symbol of the final goal of God's action. It is above history, an end which can never be completely attained on this earth. (2) Heaven also refers to the ideal possibilities latent in any particular set of actual conditions. The fulfillment of these possibilities is heaven coming to earth. Heaven, then, has a double reference. The immediate concern of visionary reason is some particular situation before us right now in all its complexity and with all its inevitable compromises. Our day-to-day task is to bring a bit of heaven to earth for somebody whenever and wherever we can, as opportunity arises. The ultimate concern of visionary reason is to form a society in which all evil has been put down. Hence, heaven is the moving image of the perfect society which lures all of life upward and forward toward that end for which God strives.

The civil rights movement led by Martin Luther King, Jr. is a good example of what I am talking about. In human affairs every now and then a situation emerges pregnant with possibilities for moral advance. Such a one emerged when Rosa Parks refused to go to the back of the bus in Montgomery. This event led to a boycott and brought King to the fore in what was the beginning of a giant leap forward for the rights of black people. Potential leaders with the abilities of King had doubtless been around before. But the times were not ready. Ideal possibilities were latent in the decade between 1958 and 1968 that had not been present before. Educational standards among blacks were rising. Thousands of black soldiers returning from World War II were unwilling to put up with segregation any longer. Racial attitudes among white people were moderating. These and many other factors had made the time ripe for a breakthrough. King and others led a series of nonviolent protests and boycotts which moved things forward. At the same time that black people were attacking the worst evils of the moment, King made his magnificent address in Washington. "I have a dream," he said, of a time when oppression will be at last ended, when white and black people will live together in peace, harmony, and justice. He used the language of the Old Testament, speaking of a pilgrim people freed from bondage in Egypt. Up to now, he said, his people had been wandering in a wilderness. But now, by the providence of God and by the militant actions of both blacks and whites, they were on their way to a promised land of equality and freedom. In saying this King had one eye on the present—doing what was required to overcome immediate oppression—and one eye on the future: the attainment of a just society. The combination was powerful in its impact.

At this point it is necessary to guard against a basic misunderstanding. The Kingdom of God is not a static end to be achieved once and for all at some definite moment in the future. Neither is it a series of such ends, one succeeding another as conditions change. Heaven is not like the mirage of an oasis in the desert that lures us on with the promise of cool water, only to turn into hot, dry sand every time we approach it. Viewed this way, life would be a sequence of failures, each moment or epoch falling short of some elusive ideal which keeps leaping ahead and beyond us. Rather, there are possibilities that *are not now being lived out* that could constitute a fuller presence of the Kingdom. Christ's promise of the Kingdom means that what is happening to us right now is offering us the gift of more abundant life than we now have. His call is that we open ourselves and use those saving possibilities in every situation. The gospel beckons us to awaken "now" to the better option. We are urged to experience the promise in the present moment as the Kingdom of God breaking in. Whatever joy there is is in the living itself, the living out or the living toward those fulfillments latent in some specific situation.

Actual life, of course, is always a mixture of good and evil, fulfillment and frustration. Moreover, progress toward the coming of heaven on earth is not a simple, easy movement upward in painless growth. It is not the case that every day in every way we all become better and better. Gradual progress does occur in many areas of life. Babies do grow up to healthy and happy adulthood. Disease is conquered step by step. The moral consciousness of a people may slowly rise over periods of time. This has happened in treatment of the mentally ill, prison reform, care of the aged, the rights of laborers, and other areas. Frequently, however, the way ahead is through crisis and revolution, death and rebirth, judgment and redemption.

Between Jesus' announcement of the coming of the Kingdom and its arrival with power stand the cross and the resurrection. The symbolic meaning of these events is that God's love suffers and triumphs in history. The crucifixion teaches us how fragile in this life goodness is. Every positive achievement can be struck down with ease. Only a Leonardo can paint a Mona Lisa; anyone at all can destroy it. But the resurrection teaches us that life has an inherent and persistent capacity to rise again after defeat, even to bring new life out of death.

The cross and resurrection are also symbols of the price of moral rebirth. We have to die to old ways of thinking, feeling, and acting before we can be reborn to a new and better self. We usually do not do so until we are faced with disaster if we continue in the old way. We cannot do so unless the new possibility becomes available. And the conversion from the old to the new is painful, a dying and rebirth. Whether we speak of the quest of individuals for health and happiness or the quest of societies for peace, prosperity, and justice, the story is the same. Paul sums it up by saying that the whole creation has been groaning in travail until now. Doubtless, as long as life remains on earth, the pain of the struggle will continue.

Nevertheless, I, with countless others, am still haunted by the ideal of perfection. It is a note that runs deep in Western thought. It has roots in Greek philosophy as well as in the Bible. Plato envisioned a Republic that reflected the Form of the perfect good. The prophets of Israel dreamed of a New Jerusalem. And in the New Testament, idealism is urgent and unqualified. It appears in the moral teachings of the Sermon on the Mount and in the promise of complete victory over evil at the end. Go the second mile. Give to everyone who would borrow. Resist not one who is evil. Turn the other cheek when struck. These sayings of Jesus require an absolute obedience expressed in acts of love for the neighbor which are impossible to carry out consistently. In fact, sometimes to refrain from resisting one who is evil would be irresponsible. It would result in much more evil than good. Nevertheless, the final promise is that when the end comes, all enemies will be put down, including death (1 Cor. 15:24-28). The holy city that comes down out of the heavens will know no sorrow, tears, pain, or death (Rev. 21:4). But impossible as these commands appear, and as remote as such a city seems, they continue to fascinate the imagination of Christians.

The faithful live between the perfection of the Biblical heaven and the stubborn, complicated facts of the actual world. The perennial problem for them is how to live joyfully before God and one another without becoming complacent about the evils on earth or despairing because the promised heaven never comes. When human hopes continually fail, and when pain, tears, death, and sorrow torment us still, the final resolution is the companionship with a divine love that suffers with us in our time of trouble. God wills for us the perfect good and works for it, although on earth the divine reach exceeds the divine grasp. We too are called into this creative venture with

God in quest of heaven. Heaven remains above and beyond any perfect achievement. Yet it is sufficiently present to make the risk of failure worthwhile and the thrill of success sweet indeed.

The task of Christians is to become sensitive to the growing edges of moral advance, and recognize where decisive action can change things for the better. Christians should be on the frontiers of human affairs looking for those right and ripe moments when ideal possibilities are ready to flower if nurtured and encouraged. To change the metaphor, they should be midwives of the Kingdom. They must help situations pregnant with moral possibilities to bring forth new life and fresh hope for God's children. The next quarter of a century leading to the year 2000 will present many such opportunities. The image of birth is a pertinent one. In poor countries the birth rate is soaring, while consumption has levelled off (which means *per capita* consumption is going down); in rich countries the birth rate has levelled off, while consumption is increasing. This not only produces horrible, inflammatory discrepancies of wealth, but also uses up the earth's resources at a rate that will eventually threaten everyone with starvation. Meeting the challenge will call for the death of some old beliefs and habits concerning nation, population, and wealth and consumption, among many others. Rebirth is possible. Redemption can follow judgment, if we are alive to the impulses of the Spirit and open to the new future God wills for us.

What does this conception of the ethics of the Kingdom imply for the mission of the church? The church came into being as the community of the end. It was created by the faith that the new age had begun. The conviction that the coming of Jesus had inaugurated the end distinguished the first Christians from the Jews. The church was made up of those who believed that the time of waiting was over and the time of fulfillment had begun. The end was no longer afar off but was now at hand. In Christ all things had become new. The church was a community of people who had been grasped by the hope of the coming Kingdom and whose love for each other bore witness to that hope. The New Testament idea of the church as a hope-filled congregation is the basis for my conception of the church as a visionary community. The task of the church is to be the bearer and nourisher of Christian visionary reason in a society increasingly dominated by technological reason.

This social task, however, does not define the basic reality of the church. The church cannot win its way by trying to outdo other institutions in offering the best solutions to worldly problems. The church, first of all, calls people to faith in God and into a new life of loving reconciliation with their Creator and with all earth's creatures. The primary task of the visionary community is to testify to its religious vision, and to celebrate the joyful life generated by it. But celebrating this life means sharing it, trying to give others the fullest possible life by interacting with them. Supreme satisfaction for the Christian is achieved when his or her life is lived in loving unity with all life, and with God's creative purpose, which wills and works for ever higher realizations of enjoyment and ecstasy. To proclaim the divine enterprise toward the fullest life for all is the church's main ministry. To take part in that enterprise—to embody its vision in its internal life of fellowship and worship—is the church's main function.

The social task of the church is to manifest its faith, outwardly and practically. Its aim should be to incorporate into the structures of individual life and society the values that express the reality of the Christian hope. The church should not suppose that *its* actions to establish these values as the rule for our secular life are what create the Kingdom. The Kingdom is there waiting and wanting to become real as the fulfillment of the purpose in the very nature of things. Our work can only allow or assist the ideal possibilities to become actual facts. The prior reality is the Kingdom hovering over history, already and partially breaking in and yet remaining above and beyond any complete consummation. The church is the community of hope. Its life is created by confidence in the reality and promise of the Kingdom's coming. The secular mission of the church to the structures of society is to clear away the obstacles that prevent life's inherent need for joy from blossoming into fulfillment. We may plant, and we may water, but God gives the increase of growth. This organic analogy expresses it perfectly. Life comes with a drive and a potentiality for enjoyment. That is God's work. Likewise, the ideal possibilities continually ahead of any present reality are God's, and are not always obvious to people. The church, however, is people firmly convinced of these "things not seen," and they must express their faith by living out its implications. Having been grasped by the promise, the community of believers must attempt in their worldly vocations to live by the values implied in their Christian vision.

The social task of the visionary community is to practice the ethics of the Kingdom. What does it mean to reproduce in our action the quality and aim of God's actions toward us in the context of an emerging postindustrial society? If the prior reality is the love of God at work in the world to make heaven real, what would it mean for Christians to reproduce that quality of love and that aim in their actions toward each other amid the threats and promises of today? The answer to these questions is basically twofold. The first part of the social mission of the visionary community is to discern the ideal possibilities that are waiting and wanting to be born. The second is to nourish these possibilities and assist them in coming to birth. The first is a matter of dreaming. The second is a matter of doing.

The future of American society will be shaped by the ways in which problem solving (knowledge), decision making (politics), and goal setting (values) interact with each other. The first contribution the church can make to our emerging cybernetic society is to create out of its heritage a vision of what a humanly desirable future would be. The church must set itself to envision the ideal society of the immediate future that is potential in the present. The church should be one of the "utopia factories" called for by Alvin Toffler.[5] For what ends were we created? What is a truly human life? What do we mean by a good person and the good life? What would an ideal society look like if it were designed to bring as much of heaven to earth as possible? What does God will and intend for the year 2000? The fundamental goal of the visionary community should be to define the meaning, purpose, destiny, and duty of human beings in the light of what has been revealed about God's intentions in the world.

Religious faith, to be sure, must make use of secular reason to create a goal for society that is both possible and practical. Even a Kingdom-inspired vision of the good future can be given flesh and blood reality only by making use of facts about what is and can be. This requirement can be met by making use of the knowledge that Christians themselves bring to the envisioning task. Vision making is a task of the whole church, not just of its theologians and professionally trained ministers. Churches are populated with assembly-line workers, corporation executives, scientists, technicians, office workers, doctors, teachers, politicians, and many others—all of whom have insight to offer about the actual world. These perspectives are essential to the nourishing of a better world.

To carry out the task both of vision making and of relating vision to vocation, we need a Spirit-inspired outburst of creative imagination that will invent appropriate institutional mechanisms. Most of these are yet to be conceived. One approach, however, might be to attempt three organizational arrangements:

1. Centers for Religion and the Future are needed at the seminary level. These Centers would bring together interdisciplinary teams of theologians, scientists, sociologists, engineers, and secular futurists of all sorts. They would keep in touch with people who are actually creating alternative futures.[6] The task of these Centers would be to study specific institutions and patterns in our society and to make down-to-earth, practical suggestions for living responsibly in this complicated world. The work of the Centers would be communicated to a larger public. They would seek to involve as many ordinary people as possible of every race, class, and region in the goal-setting and strategy-devising process. It is not essential that all seminaries establish such Centers. A few strategically located ones might choose this task as their special contribution to the life of the church. Those that do choose to go this direction need not establish an independent Center if adjunct relationships can be worked out with nearby univer-

sities to provide the specialized resources that would be needed. Numerous future-oriented institutes have appeared in the past decade. Their personnel and findings might be tapped for the specific use of religiously oriented futurists.

Consider an example of what such a center could do. Every alert citizen knows that the world is in a race between growing numbers of people and available food. The United States will unavoidably have some hard choice to make, since we are the world's major exporter of grain. Economic factors, moral compassion, and political realities will be intermixed. Nothing is more fundamental than the Christian imperative to feed the hungry. But providing food to the starving in our world is a complicated affair, requiring both the warm heart and the cool head. Meeting major world problems involves a combination of problem-solving knowledge, political decision making, and value choices. A Center for Religion and the Future could serve the church and the Christian conscience by studying the problem of world hunger. It would take these factors into account in its inquiries. Conclusions arrived at would be made available for public discussion and action. No problem will tax our knowledge, our politics, and our morality in the next quarter of a century more than hunger. What will the churches do about it?

2. At the regional and congregational levels, ecumenical and denominational ministries must bring people together in laboratories of reflection. Such laboratories would provide a forum where Christian visions could be correlated with the responsibilities of everyday life. The focus of concern here would be to help each Christian learn how to function as an agent of the kingdom in the main institution with which he or she is involved. This might be factory, office, laboratory, school, hospital, home, or some other organization. On a weekend study retreat several men reported the tensions they faced in their jobs. All of them helped produce materials used for bombing North Vietnam. As Christians they were morally opposed to the war. Can we create support groups in the churches which will help people work through the many conflicts they face every day between their Christian values

and the requirements of their jobs? Can churches equip those of their members who hold decision-making authority in institutions to act on moral principles expressive of Christian visionary reason? Providing a forum in which Christians can gather with Christians facing similar problems would be a tremendous contribution.

I have no illusion that it is easy for Christians to challenge the organizations for which they work. It is difficult and risky. Jobs and careers are at stake. "Don't rock the boat" is the philosophy most managers and owners would like to have their employees follow. Most of us know people who, when they raised a question about some morally questionable practice, were told to mind their own business "or else." Consider physicians who would like to see their professional organization become more concerned about delivering health care to the poor and less single-mindedly bent on self-interest. They usually end up belonging to an isolated minority. Executives of large corporations may be, as individuals, decent people and loyal church members. But when they function in their jobs, they are caught up in pressures to increase corporate profits that often stifle their moral impulses. And if conscience troubles them at all, they rationalize by saying, "What is good for General Motors is good for the country." Similarly, those in positions of lesser authority fall into "small-time Eichmannism." Eichmann, tried in Israel as a Nazi war criminal, admitted that he murdered untold thousands of Jews, but said that he was only following orders from higher up. He protested that he was powerless to do otherwise.

Paul wrote that we battle not against flesh and blood but against principalities and powers. The "principalities and powers" of today, with truly demonic capacity, are the huge organizations that force their standards and practices upon people caught up in them. Kind-hearted military men in the U.S. and U.S.S.R. are led to argue for more and more powerful weapons of destruction. They are not bad people as individuals. Yet their folly may kill us all. They are caught up in a deadly contest whose rules are only partially made by themselves. They feel they are only doing what they have to. So it is throughout government bureaus, corporation offices, labor unions, retail stores, small business firms, and so on. People work in a network of forces and standards which they did not create and cannot as individuals destroy. So they feel helpless to change them. Their security and the welfare of their families are dependent on their keeping their jobs. Who wants to bite the hand that feeds him? Is it not idle talk to speak of church members living out their Christian visionary reason in these situations? Possibly. But on the other side it is *certainly* idle to speak of living a responsible Christian life without at least raising the question of how we should connect faith in God and the ethics of organizations. It is these organizations that do our work, meet our material needs, and affect the quality of life of us all.

3. Finally, we need task forces at every level of church life that will focus on a specific sector of society. These task forces would ask about Christian responsibilities in the light of careful, critical analysis of what is actually going on. The issues are many: poverty, prison reform, pollution, racial justice, women's rights, energy policy, foreign policy, world hunger, among others. Task forces of this sort are nothing new. One example is found in the Rochester, New York, area. Genesee Ecumenical Ministries is coodinating the efforts of several denominations to alleviate the problems of judicial process. This project was given special impetus by the revolt at nearby Attica prison. That tragic event took a terrible toll of human life and brought the problem to the attention of the whole community in a forceful way. Task forces are springing up at many levels of church life to deal with the crisis of world hunger. It takes but a little imagination to see how a wide variety of resources could be coordinated and brought to bear on any number of such issues.

Not all Christians will come to the same conclusions or agree upon the same strategies. Equally devoted believers can be found all across the political and social spectrum. Some think that capitalism was born in heaven. Others think that socialism is the only path to utopia. Some are pro-abortion, given certain circumstances. Some think abortion is murder. The variety of moral opinions among Christians is a problem. There is, however, something worse than that. Frequently the views of Christians do not represent honest conclusions based on hard reflection over the implications of Christian morality. Rather, they reflect the mind-set characteristic of their race or region or economic class or occupation. The main purpose of the laboratories of reflection and the task forces would not be to arrive at unanimity of opinion. Rather, it would be to give integrity to the effort to connect religious faith and social practice.

Many visions flourish in the Christian community regarding the task to which the Spirit is calling the churches. My proposal is admittedly not representative of the mood and mentality that prevails in many segments of the church today. These other claims also respond to felt needs and have their own legitimacy and constituencies. The activist impulse does not beat as strongly as it did a few years ago. After a period of experimentation during the turmoil of the 1960s, the mainline denominations are in a period of retrenchment, belt tightening, and rethinking. The turn is inward. The shift has been from world to church, from remaking the society to nurturing the spiritual resources of individuals and families. Revitalizing the inner life of persons and congregations is a major focus of interest. The coming years will likely see those groups with a more liberal, socially active outlook growing weaker in money, numbers, and zeal. More conservative, evangelistically oriented churches are among the fastest growing. The gap between change-oriented, social-action Christians and status quo-oriented, individual-holiness ones may even widen. In any case, the debate over the meaning and purpose of the church in relation to social structures and problems will probably continue to divide us.

This book has not been written to speak to the current mood. It is an attempt to look at long-term trends. In response to the needs of the coming years, I am proposing a mission that has authentic roots in the Biblical view of God's purpose and people. The intent is not to be popular. It is, rather, to be a faithful witness to one accent with which the Spirit is speaking to the churches of today and tomorrow.

In the final chapter I want to get very specific about some opportunities that are emerging in our time. Christian visionary reason should nourish them and bring them to birth by individual and corporate action.

CHAPTER 6

A Declaration of Interdependence

What does it mean to be a morally responsible citizen in a complicated world? This is the question to which this book has been addressed. Its intention has been to describe the setting in which moral thinking must go on in the coming years. A further aim has been to suggest an ethical perspective based on the Bible. My purpose has not been to provide ready-made, prepackaged answers. Nevertheless, some of my own convictions about what Christians and churches should do with respect to particular political and economic questions have been clearly implicit in these pages. In this last chapter, it seems appropriate to develop a few of them more fully. I do so in order to give some specific illustrations of how visionary reason might respond to the challenges of today and tomorrow. The proposals I make also point out some problems that might be dealt with in a Center for religion and the future. These problems, of course, would also be appropriate for laboratories of reflection and task forces in churches to deal with. Finally, the material provided could be used to show how problem solving, decision making, and goal setting must all be taken into account in dealing with moral problems in a cybernetic society.

I invite the reader to think through certain issues with me. Some will agree; others will disagree. My aim is to present conclusions I have come to, along with some of the facts and reasons that have led me to them. I know full well that there are opposing arguments and evidence that lead to different convictions about what ought to be done. Much of what I will say has been implicit in the previous chapters, and it seems only fair that I "come clean" and declare myself openly. No reader is likely to be surprised by what appears in these concluding pages. If I appear to be a crusader in behalf of certain controversial political and economic views, I do so deliberately. My purpose, however, is not to give dogmatic answers to complex problems but to stimulate discussion. I invite rebuttal. What is important is that we all think deeply and realistically about our responsibility in the light of the moral imperatives of Biblical religion. I am not so much concerned that everyone agree with me as I am that all get involved and commit themselves to what their own visionary reason tells them to do. Hence, I urge the reader to enter into conversation about America and the future of humankind.

The century beyond 1976 will take us into a future that will be different from the past. We are viewing the convulsive birth pangs of a planetary society pregnant with unprecedented promise and peril. The world stands in need of a vision of its destiny as a unified global community of interdependent human beings. We inhabit a potentially bountiful and benign but also possibly vulnerable and virulent Spaceship Earth. Do the moral resources for meeting the challenge of the future lie in a combination of American ideals and Biblical religion? The United States has great material wealth and power. We have enormous, expanding resources of scientific knowledge and technical know-how that could be used for meeting human needs. We have in our heritage a belief in freedom and a dream of justice for all. A reservoir of idealism resides in the hearts of ordinary Americans. As we enter the third century of our history, is there any hope at all for inaugurating a Second American Revolution?

What would a Second American Revolution mean? One idea certainly must be in the center of any vision of a desirable future: equality. It is an ideal basic to both American history and Biblical religion.

EQUALITY

Jesus	*The Declaration of Independence*
You shall love your neighbor as yourself. (Lev. 19:18; Luke 10:27)	All men are created equal.

Jesus taught his followers to regard their neighbor's need as equal to their own. In today's world the neighbor is, in principle, any human being in need. The Declaration of Independence was a political document that marked a great step forward. It must be read against the background of the divine right of kings and the absolute power assumed by governments. Viewed in that context, the statement that every human being has certain inalienable rights given by God that governments and kings cannot take away is a remarkable claim. After two centuries we are still trying to live out the implications of that creed. In the beginning it was mainly white, property-owning males who were really equal. In the Constitution, before it was amended, a black slave counted as 3/5 of a person in determining how many representatives a state would have in Congress. It took nearly a century to outlaw slavery. After another century we are still far from achieving racial equality. Women were not given the right to vote until the 20th century. The Constitutional amendment to guarantee equal rights for women ran into strong opposition throughout the country. In many areas of our common life women are still discriminated against by law and by custom. In the early days, only those (white males) who owned a certain amount of property could vote. Nevertheless, the ideal of equality was declared. It has a validity for political, economic, and social life that we are still working on.

Equality as a legal principle and as a moral ideal has never meant that there are no differences of intelligence, physical prowess, talent, or virtue among people. In all such particulars the human race exhibits great variety. The meaning is that every human being has the same rights to life, liberty, and the pursuit of happiness. All are equal before the law. Each person has the same claim to the means of human fulfillment as any other, no more and no less. In religious terms equality means that God loves all earthborn children alike. Every person is of infinite worth. God has no preferences of race, religion, sex, or nation. A person is a person. The moral requirement to love other people equally with oneself is an implication of the love of God which goes out to all human beings without favoritism.

A Declaration of Interdependence is needed to further universalize the principle of equality. The idea that everybody counts for one and nobody counts for more than one must now be applied to the realities and possibilities of Spaceship Earth. Two implications of equality and interdependence come into view at once. (1) The economic system and the tax laws are stacked in favor of the wealthy, the powerful, and the few. A political movement is needed to unite poor and moderate income groups. The aim should be to redress the balance for the sake of a more equal distribution of power and wealth. (2) The resources of the whole world must, in the long run, be regarded as belonging to all the people of the earth. The massive inequalities of wealth and consumption that now divide the rich countries from the poor countries are morally intolerable. The ideal that all people should have equal access to the material means of human fulfillment should be a goal toward which we move as fast as opportunity, prudence, and political reality allow. The most feasible path toward such an ideal is to incorporate into the structure of economic life the actual interdependence of the world's people. The more immediate need is for economic aid to underdeveloped countries, along with famine relief in emergency situations.

The nearest I ever came to engaging in a deliberate act of civil disobedience was about a decade ago when I read *The Great Treasury Raid* by Philip M. Stern.[1] This book tells how the tax laws of this country have been manipulated by wealthy people and huge corporations for their own interests and to the disadvantage of the large majority of less privileged citizens. I threatened to refuse to pay my income taxes in protest of this outrageous situation. The other part of my plan was to denounce the unfair tax advantages I received as a minister. Either prudence or cowardice finally prevailed, and I backed down. Nonetheless, my sense of outrage is still present. Wealth and power are unequally and unfairly distributed in America today. This injustice is built into the system itself. I will not try to prove that claim in a paragraph. A good deal of the evidence in available in two books to which I refer the interested reader: *A Populist Manifesto* by Jack Newfield and Jeff Greenfield and *The Rape of the Taxpayer* by Philip Stern.[2]

If the average American can read the first chapter of Mr. Stern's more recent book and not be red with anger, then I am at a loss as to what would stir indignation. Consider chapter 19, "Letter from an Indignant Taxpayer." This is a letter actually sent on August 9, 1972, by Philip Stern's secretary to Chairman Wilbur Mills of the House Ways and Means Committee and to Chairman Russell Long of the Senate Finance Committee. The letter tells what she has learned by typing Stern's book at a salary of $150 a week. On the $7,800 she earned in 1971, she paid federal income taxes of $1,057.50. She asks why she has to pay nearly 14% of her earnings when some millionaries get off for practically nothing. Granted the case of J. Paul Getty is an extreme one, but it certainly impressed Ms. Saunders. He is said to be worth over a billion dollars and reportedly earned up to $300,000 a day during the early sixties. Yet from what President Kennedy told two senators, Getty paid only a few thousand dollars in tax. She goes on to recite instance after instance, all documented in her boss' book, of loopholes that favor the rich. She also reminds Senator Long of how insistent he has been that welfare recipients ought to do a minimum of work. They might, he suggests, clean up "their filthy neighborhoods." Why, then, is Mr. Long not bothered by the fact that those who get what amounts to a free gift in tax savings are not required to do any work? Specially-privileged capital gains and tax-free municipal bonds are prime examples of work-free welfare. She proceeds to ask similar questions about the billions that corporations like General Motors and IBM will save over a period of years by investment credit and such wonders as "asset depreciation range." Mr. Stern shows how very weak the case is for these bonanzas. Ms. Saunders admits that she doesn't fully understand all the complexities of the tax laws. But she did learn some of the usual defenses of these profitable schemes. She concludes that most of the reasoning is rationalization for a rip-off. Stern's book documents the claim that the real welfare programs in this country are for the rich, not for the poor.

In June of 1974 the news media reported a swindle that illustrates how the law protects the very rich. About 2,000 wealthy investors poured $130 million into a scheme to drill oil wells. About $100 million of it disappeared. Home-Stake Production Company of Tulsa lured these well-heeled speculators into a deal crammed with tax benefits. Tax shelters enable people in high income brackets to invest money that would otherwise go to the IRS. By investing in a business such as oil drilling, they earn income that is protected from taxation by lucrative allowances. A whole industry has come into being to exploit every nook and cranny of these quite legal tax shelters. Despite the swindle, the lucrative benefits of the law will insure that those who invested huge amounts will probably end up with little loss.

According to Philip Stern, America's richest 3,000 families get an average of $720,000 in tax welfare. The time has come for thoroughgoing tax reform. The basic principle of such reform is stated in the Sixteenth Amendment to the Constitution which instituted the income tax. This Amendment gives Congress the power to tax income "from whatever source derived." Put otherwise, the idea would be "to stop treating money earned through prior wealth more favorably than that earned through hard work."[3] Closing the loopholes would make a difference of $77 billion a year, according to Stern. How can there be equality before the law until the income tax scandal is corrected?

If millions of average taxpayers are being subjected annually to such unfairness, why don't they rise up and vote out the lawmakers who allow this outrage to go on? Many people don't know the facts. Others are resigned to the fact that "the little guy will always get it in the neck." Some may secretly envy the rich. Others simply may not care. Seldom do the politicians offer much of an alternative at election time. Those in Congress who are in favor of tax reform have difficulty getting on the right committees. The sheer complexity of tax laws is a barrier to reforming them. A major reason tax reform is so hard to come by is that representatives and senators are financed heavily by contributions from the wealthy who benefit from the present tax structure. Who is foolish enough to bite the hand that feeds him? Even the Watergate and related scandals which showed dramatically how money corrupts power have so far produced only minor ripples in the direction of reforming campaign financing. However, the political power is there if middle and lower income citizens would unite and combine their efforts.

Inequality in the distribution of wealth and income is a closely related issue. The ratio of the total national income going to the poorest and the richest segments of society has changed little over the last quarter of a century. Yet the total output of goods more than doubled between 1947 and 1970. The actual figures for 1970 are:[4]

Poorest fifth	5.5%
Second fifth	12.0
Third fifth	17.4
Fourth fifth	23.5
Richest fifth	41.6

These are before-tax incomes. But the so-called progressive income tax changes those proportions only a few points. The after-tax share is nearly as unbalanced as it is before the IRS gets its portion. The stated tax rates range from 14% to 70%. The actual rates are quite different. The average rate for taxpayers in the $50,000 to $75,000 range in 1971 was 22%. For those earning over a million dollars a year, the average rate was only 32%. On the whole, the rate of taxation is roughly proportional to income, except for the richest 5% of the population.[5] These percentages take on more meaning when it is recognized that 90% of American families lived on incomes of less than $13,000 after taxes in 1970.[6]

Isn't this the land of equal opportunity? Don't the differences in income reflect what people deserve in terms of their effort, talent, and total contribution to the country? These are only partial truths. Great opportunities do exist for the resourceful, the hard working, and the ambitious. Those who make a greater contribution perhaps deserve a greater reward. Nevertheless, the present arrangements in America developed over two centuries have created built-in advantages for some, disadvantages for others. Those with great wealth and power keep the cards stacked in their favor. Children simply do not start off with an equal chance in present society. Moreover, the present wealth of America and its future capacity for producing goods and services have been built up over many years by the brains and brawn of many people. Hence, it is impossible to justify any continuation of the present inequalities. Wealth is a social product. Black slaves as well as gifted inventors like Henry Ford, the work of millions of ordinary citizens as well as of entrepreneurs like John D. Rockefeller have made America rich and powerful. The present reward system is out of proportion to present contributions, given the unfair advantage with which the children of the privileged begin. Youths who start off poor do occasionally make millions. But these exceptions do not modify the big picture very much. There are no simple answers to questions of fair play in such complicated matters as this. Nevertheless, a redistribution of wealth in the direction of greater equality is one major move that interdependence demands.

Income redistribution can be accomplished. We know how to do it. An estimate of two or three years ago was that a reallocation of only 5% of the total national income would bring every family up to a minimum of $5,000 a year.[7] A shift in this direction could be brought about by providing grants to individuals or families sufficient to allow a minimal standard of living. This system could totally replace the present system, which nearly everyone agrees is a "welfare mess." A number of proposals have been made along this line. Both conservative and liberal politicians have spoken in favor of the idea. The administrations of President Nixon and of President Ford have considered welfare revisions of this type. Schemes may go under the heading of Negative Income Tax or Guaranteed Annual Income. Basically their aim is to provide a guaranteed floor of income for everybody. Providing a minimum of $3,600 for a family of four would add $25 billion to the government's budget. A floor of $5,500 would cost $71 billion.[8] How would it be paid for? First of all, we could reduce spending in other areas. A substantial body of responsible expert opinion in this country maintains that the nation could defend itself on a budget of $20 billion less. Second, we could adopt a no-nonsense, no-loophole income tax with steeply graduated rates set at whatever levels were required to pay for the agreed family minimum.[9]

A number of income redistribution plans have been proposed. Dr. Harold W. Watts, for example, presented a scheme in 1972 to the Democratic Platform Committee which has much merit.[10] It would replace the whole system of present public assistance programs and individual income tax schedules. No typical family of four would have less than $3,720. Work incentives would apply at every income level. Any person making less than $50,000 would keep at least $2 of every $3 earned. Nobody would keep less than 50¢ of every dollar earned. Only 3 out of every 10 people would end up with less than they have now. Put differently, 70% of the entire population would have more than they do. Moreover, the total revenue paid to the government would increase by $3 billion. These figures would need to be adjusted for today's conditions and incomes. Nevertheless, Dr. Watts' plan indicates what is feasible.

Many understandably balk at what seems to be giving money to people, no strings attached. However, we already allow a deduction of $750 for each person. An exemption or deduction amounts in effect to a grant in terms of reduced taxes. The present system "gives" more to the rich than it does to those of moderate or low incomes. For a family of four paying on a 14% tax schedule, the $750 individual deduction provides a savings in taxes of $420. A wealthy family paying at the 70% rate saves $2,100. Moreover, we already give welfare to those who have little or no income at all. Some critics claim that a guaranteed annual income would destroy motivation, corrupt character, and create an army of welfare loafers. This is not very likely. If a person making $50,000 feels that $10,000 more a year is enough incentive to change jobs (and people in such cases almost invariably do), then it would seem that a father would find four mouths to feed enough incentive to look for work, even if he had $5,000 guaranteed to him. A person who will not work in order to get more than $5,000 to support a family at today's prices may have problems, but it is hardly lack of incentive. A Department of Labor report issued in June of 1974 indicated that a typical family of four living in a city required $8,200 for an "austere" budget and $12,600 for a "moderate" one. The requirements for a moderate budget had risen $1,200 in one year because of inflation.

The issue of income redistribution is a splendid example of

the way problem-solving knowledge, politics, and values interact to determine the direction of society. Economists and tax specialists may invent various plans and specify the costs, benefits, and consequences of each. No plan can be instituted, however, unless the political power can be mustered in Congress to pass the legislation and persuade the president to sign it. Fundamental also are the attitudes and values involved. Right now there is probably not enough sentiment in favor of economic equality and redistribution of wealth to make use of the knowledge or to mobilize the political power. Should not Christians in their roles as citizens and voters take the lead in creating the political possibility for income redistribution? Should not churches in their corporate witness take the lead in developing attitudes and values favorable to equalization of opportunity and privilege? Here is something immediate and practical that Christians and churches can do. They can help create the moral climate and the political realities that will make income redistribution both possible and necessary.

The meaning of the ideal of equality at the global level is more difficult by far. The claim that the resources of the whole world belong to the people of the whole world is an implication of the doctrine of creation as stated in Psalm 24:1: "The earth is the LORD'S and the fulness thereof, the world and those who dwell therein." However, between that ultimate goal of religious faith and the immediate historical facts stand numerous secondary principles. Chief among them are the territorial and property rights of individuals and nations. The United Nations should not, even if they could, immediately take over the oil of Saudi Arabia for general distribution to all alike. Nor should the wheatfields of Kansas at once be declared a commons from which all can harvest indiscriminately. A request this year from the Eskimos for their share of General Motors should not be honored.

Nevertheless, we need to enlarge our moral vision beyond national boundaries. In the decades ahead all peoples of the earth will move toward a converging destiny. It has taken two centuries for us to *begin* to live out the meaning of the declaration that "all men are created equal" in our own country. It may take two more centuries before we put into practice the global ideal of equality. Two things can be said, however, about the immediate practicalities of achieving this goal.

1. The world is being knit together in bonds of economic interdependence. This is a hopeful sign. Those who depend on each other and know it are more likely to play fair. Increased trade between the U.S.S.R. and the U.S. may be a step toward warming relations between them. It may even turn them away from the madness of the arms race. There is hope in the fact that some of the nonindustrial countries do have rich resources. This gives them a potential base of power. We have seen what the Arab countries can do with the threat of oil embargoes. Nevertheless, the system of world trade is still stacked in favor of the rich countries, just as economic opportunities in America are stacked in favor of those who already have wealth. It is an obvious truism that ideals flourish best when they can be connected with the mutual self-interests of interacting parties. Where interests do not merge, justice treads a more tortuous path. Moral idealism in this case can only moderate the baser passions of nations.

2. The rich countries must assist the poorer countries for immediate humanitarian reasons and for the long-range reasons of global peace and security. Masses of impoverished and desperate people are a threat to everybody's future. Here is a point at which Christians and churches can do something immediately in a down-to-earth practical way to help the wretched of the earth. Former Secretary of Defense Robert McNamara, now head of the World Bank, recently reminded a conference of religious leaders how desperate is the plight of millions of the world's poor. 800 million people live on 30 cents a day or less. In parts of the underdeveloped countries 25% of all children die before they are five years old. Life expectancy is at least 20 years shorter in these countries than in America. He went on to say that only 3% of the expected economic growth of this country through 1980 would be required to meet the United Nations' goal of .7% of GNP (gross national product) devoted to assistance funds. We now contribute only .125%. This percentage puts us 14th among the 16 developed coun-

tries in the giving of aid. Edward P. Morgan gave figures to show how little we now do in this regard. We spend $20 billion for alcoholic beverages, $13 billion for cigarettes, $5 billion for cosmetics, and $3.5 billion for aid to developing countries. Mr. McNamara, speaking as a Presbyterian elder, said, "If the churches will not speak to these issues, who will?"

James Grant, president of the Overseas Development Council, pointed out that the myth of producing more in order that all may have enough is being shattered. The earth has limited resources. We are realizing that there are ecological limits to growth. Inevitably, then, emphasis must shift from production to distribution. Global justice has to do with a more equal sharing of the world's goods. Redistribution will require not only a new politics but new life-styles emphasizing reduced consumption and conservation. Religious communities can play a large part, Grant said, in preparing for an era of scarcity.

Lester Brown claimed that famine is shifting from geography to economics. The poor in every nation are going to be caught in the squeeze. There are radical shifts going on in our world that mark a transition from one global era to another. The movement is from production to distribution, from supply to demand, from independence to interdependence. To emphasize present inequalities, he pointed out that the average American uses 150 times more energy than the average Nigerian. The great question before the world is not simply how to produce more but how to distribute what we have more equitably. This means, Brown said, that the problem has shifted from the domain of economists to that of theologians.[11]

There are hungry people in the world today. More empty stomachs are likely in the years to come. What will the churches do? I have spoken of the problem of values in this book. In real life that comes down to asking what prosperous Americans will do in the presence of the bloated bellies and shriveling bodies of children whose helpless parents have only love but no food to offer them. I have spoken of the church as the bearer of Christian visionary reason. In practical terms, that means envisioning a world in which there is no hunger and asking what must be done beginning right now to realize that dream. One immediate task of Christian visionary reason would be to mobilize the moral energies of Christian people in support of greatly increased economic assistance to the countries in which millions of people literally do not know where the next meal is coming from. If we can spend nearly $100 billion for military purposes, can we not spend at least $10 billion to save people from starving? Individual Christians can write their representatives and senators in Congress letting them know that they would like to see our priorities changed. They can demand a reduction in unnecessary and wasteful military spending which an insatiable Pentagon would force on us. They can let their leaders know of their concern for the poor of the world and of their willingness to pay the needed taxes and to reduce personal consumption or do whatever it takes to make humanitarian policies possible.

Americans have grown cynical about foreign aid programs. Much of the disillusionment is justified. An intensive seven-month investigation by Donald L. Bartlett and James B. Steele reveals some of the negative aspects of past efforts.[12] More than $172 billion has been spent since World War II in overseas assistance. The authors note the following unintended consequences of what was billed as humanitarian aid to the poor. Foreign aid has:

- —Aggravated food shortages in some countries; reliance on food imports from the United States has discouraged home production.
- —Subsidized sweatshop factories and textile mills in South Korea; instead of raising standards of living, as was intended, the sweatshops have lowered it, paying from 10 to 30 cents an hour.
- —Entrenched the rich and powerful in foreign countries by aiding businesses controlled by them, thus widening instead of narrowing the gap between the rich and poor.
- —Generated windfall profits for business and financial interests in this country.
- —Led to the building of a gaming lodge in Kenya and a luxury hotel in Haiti with $150-a-day rooms, whereas the intent was to stimulate private investment that would aid the poor.

- —Created a powerful foreign-aid lobby in this country made up of corporations, financial institutions, colleges, and others who benefit by funds appropriated for overseas relief.

The authors also report that American aid has fed the hungry and provided medical assistance for the ill. It has built highways, factories, hospitals, and schools. It has financed the education of thousands of foreigners in the United States. Like all human ventures, foreign aid is flawed with greed, corruption, and mismanagement. It is a mixture of good and bad. However, we must avoid complacency and cynicism in the face of the negative side of foreign assistance. Instead, the American people should demand a thoroughgoing reconstruction of the whole range of aid programs. Once set up, they must be monitored carefully to insure that their intent is carried out. Should not Christians take the lead in demanding that humanitarian policies be legislated and rigorously enforced in the interest of lifting the wretched of the earth out of their misery?

It would be a denial of every premise in this book to claim that relieving the poverty of the world is an easy matter. Moreover, despite its wealth and power, the United States alone cannot save the world, even if it set out to do so with the purest of motives. Realism and modesty must mark all our efforts. Yet we can alleviate hunger and suffering in substantial ways if we are wise as well as compassionate. We cannot make the world perfect, but we can make it better than it is. The eminent economist, Gunnar Myrdal, makes five important points in his book *The Challenge of World Poverty*.

1. Lifting the wretched of the earth out of their misery will require a combination of thoroughgoing economic and political reforms in the poor countries and substantial aid from the developed countries. It is crucial that the developing nations take radical measures to democratize and equalize their societies. This is essential if economic advances are to benefit the masses and not simply a few.

2. Western nations have so far not made any real sacrifices to aid the world's poor. On the whole, they have not been pre-

pared to forgo even minor trade advantages that offended their long-range self-interests. Furthermore, Americans who think they are the only ones who have given assistance or believe that the United States has given more than its fair share are mistaken.

3. The aid policies of the United States have been shaped primarily to further military and political interests, not to help the impoverished masses. Humanitarian impulses have sometimes been involved, but all too frequently this country has propped up repressive and corrupt regimes under the guise of saving people from the wicked communists.

4. A new philosophy of assistance must be directed first at reforms in the interests of the poverty-stricken masses. Only in this way can aid policies escape the understandable cynicism which so many people have about them.

5. Based on this study of the facts, Myrdal concludes that "only by appealing to peoples' moral feelings will it be possible to create the popular basis for increasing aid to underdeveloped countries as substantially as it is needed."[13]

Especially noteworthy are points four and five. Point four would appeal to the revolutionary ideals on which this nation was founded. It would put us back on the side of those movements in the world which are striving for equality. I am writing these words on Independence Day, and I can hear people celebrating from my window. But it frequently happens that those who are most enthusiastic about the revolution of 1776 are the most convinced conservatives today. It is time we captured the best of our own past for the sake of all the world's oppressed. Americans in recent years have been given spurious, dishonest, and inadequate reasons for supporting aid. Widespread support on the part of Americans must be based on morally sound as well as politically realistic principles, freed from the myths and corruption of the past. Point five is a special challenge to Christians. Should not churches take the lead in appealing to the moral feelings of people?

To conclude, here are some specific things Christians can do as individuals in their roles as citizens and voters. They can:

1. Demand that their political leaders enact a no-nonsense, no-loophole income tax system which insures that all pay their fair share.

2. Urge the replacement of the present welfare system with a guaranteed minimal family income plan. The goal should be to provide an income floor for each family which is at least one-half of the median family income for the country as a whole for that particular year. This move should be coupled with other measures designed to equalize economic opportunities and benefits for every American.

3. Urge Congress and the president to work toward the goal of committing 1% of the gross national product to the assistance of the poverty-stricken countries. An aid program should be based on realistic humanitarian principles. It should be rigorously monitored to prevent corruption and misuse of funds. Aid should be made available in ways that encourage the recipient countries to make reforms which will guarantee that the masses of the poor are actually helped.

When examined, all three of these proposals raise complex issues. Nevertheless, they suggest a direction and a goal. A Declaration of Interdependence focused on the meaning of equality for the nation and the globe is one way of uniting American ideals with Biblical imperatives. Whether the time is right for a transformation of values and goals on the scale needed, I do not know. A Harris survey released in 1974 may have some significance for our topic.[14] It indicates that there are shifts in attitudes and outlook that may signal a readiness for change. The survey indicates that 59% of the American people feel alienated. This is up from 29% in 1966, and the rise has been steady. The newspaper reports that "a majority of every single major segment of the population is turned off by politics, the fairness of the economic system, and the role accorded the individual in society." From the Vietnam War through rising inflation and unemployment, to Watergate, the index of disaffection has moved upward. In 1972, 66% of blacks but only 47% of whites were basically discontented. Only two years later the percentage of white discontent had risen to 57%, while the black index remained the same. For the first time the college-educated, the suburban dwellers, and those with incomes over $15,000 have shown a majority of their members in the unhappy group. Disenchantment among young people has increased from 46% to 62% in the last two years. This is a greater rise than was evident in the late sixties and early seventies. It is not clear what all these figures mean or portend for the future. They do suggest that easy optimism cannot be sold today. They may also signal a potential responsiveness to leaders with a positive vision that is both realistic and hopeful. Disenchantment, however, can also be exploited by reactionary forces and demagogues. Alienation and disaffection only signal a readiness for change. They do not guarantee that the change will be creative.

Given this peril and prospect, what is to be the response of Christians and of churches as we celebrate the 200th birthday of the Declaration of Independence? The answer is not finally to be given in a book. We cannot, by merely taking thought, bring in a better tomorrow. The test will come in our actions; everything we do—or don't do—affects the world, so we must work cooperatively, wisely, and humanely to realize on earth the Kingdom Christ promised.

Notes

Chapter 1: Is There Any Hope?

1. Garrett Hardin, "Lifeboat Ethics: The Case Against Helping the Poor," *Psychology Today* (September 1974), pp. 38ff.
2. Robert Heilbroner, *An Inquiry into the Human Prospect* (New York: W. W. Norton & Co., 1974).
3. *The Christian Science Monitor* (June 5, 1974), p. 1.
4. Donella H. Meadows et al., *The Limits to Growth* (Washington, D. C.: Potomac Associates, 1972).
5. Lester Brown, "Rich Countries and Poor in a Finite, Interdependent World," *Daedalus* (Fall 1973), pp. 153ff.
6. Lester Brown, "Global Food Insecurity," *The Futurist* (April 1974), pp. 56ff.
7. *Rochester Democrat and Chronicle* (May 30, 1974), p. 2A.
8. See, for example, Peter Passell and Leonard Ross, *The Retreat from Riches* (New York: The Viking Press, 1973).

Chapter 2: The Future Is Not What It Used to Be

1. Herman Kahn and Anthony J. Wiener, *The Year 2000* (New York: The Macmillan Co., 1967).
2. Daniel Bell, *The Coming of Post-Industrial Society* (New York: Basic Books, Inc., 1973).
3. Peter Drucker, *The Age of Discontinuity* (New York: Harper & Row, Publishers, 1969). See also John Kenneth Galbraith, *The New Industrial State*, 2d ed., rev., (Boston: Houghton Mifflin Co., 1971).
4. Victor Ferkiss, *Technological Man* (New York: George Braziller, 1969).
5. In recognition of the centrality of electronic technologies, Zbigniew Brzezinski has named the coming period "the technetronic era." See his *Between Two Ages* (New York: The Viking Press, 1970).
6. Daniel Bell, "Notes on the Post-Industrial Society" I, *The Public Interest* (Winter 1967), pp. 24-35.

7. For examples of current futurology, see Herman Kahn and Anthony J. Wiener, *The Year 2000,* and Herman Kahn and B. Bruce-Briggs, *Things to Come: Thinking About the Seventies and Eighties* (New York: The Macmillan Co., 1972).
8. Daniel Bell, "Notes on the Post-Industrial Society" II, *The Public Interest* (Spring 1967), pp. 102-118.
9. The literature on cybernetics and systems analysis is vast. I will here mention only four works. Norbert Wiener, *The Human Use of Human Beings* (Garden City, N. Y.: Doubleday & Co., 1954; New York: Avon Books [paper], 1967); Karl Deutsch et al., *The Nerves of Government* (New York: The Free Press, 1963); Kenneth Boulding, *The Organizational Revolution* (New York: Harper & Brothers, 1953; Chicago: Quadrangle Books [paper], 1968); Ludwig von Bertalanffy, *General Systems Theory* (New York: George Braziller, 1968).
10. A theoretical framework which could be used to undergird the conception of society and its workings assumed here is found in Warren Breed, *The Self-Guiding Society* (New York: The Free Press, 1971). This book is a summation of a much larger work of Amitai Etzioni, *The Active Society* (New York: The Free Press, 1968).
11. John Platt, "What We Must Do," *Science* (November 28, 1969), pp. 1115-1121.
12. R. Buckminster Fuller, *Utopia or Oblivion* (New York: Bantam Books [paper], 1969; Overlook Press, 1972).
13. Jack Newfield and Jeff Greenfield, *A Populist Manifesto* (New York: Praeger Publishers, 1972; Warner Paperback Library, 1972).
14. Charles Reich, *The Greening of America* (New York: Random House, 1970; Bantam Books [paper], 1971).
15. Philip Slater, *The Pursuit of Loneliness* (Boston: Beacon Press, 1970 [Beacon Paperback, 1971]).
16. Theodore Roszak, *The Making of a Counter Culture* (Garden City, N. Y.: Doubleday & Co., 1969 [Anchor paperback, 1969]).

Chapter 3: Technology: Master or Servant?

1. Among the many examples that might be chosen, see Roderick Seidenberg, *Posthistoric Man* (Chapel Hill: University of North Carolina Press, 1950); Jacques Ellul, *The Technological Society*, trans. John Wilkinson (New York: Alfred A. Knopf, 1964); Lewis Mumford, *The Myth of the Machine* (New York: Harcourt, Brace & World, 1967) and *The Pentagon of Power* (New York: Harcourt, Brace, Jovanovich, Inc., 1970); Theodore Roszak, *The Making of a Counter Culture* (Garden City, N. Y.: Doubleday & Co., 1969 [Anchor paperback, 1969]); Erich Fromm, *The Revolution of Hope* (New York: Harper & Row, Publishers, 1968; Bantam Books [paper], 1968). Cf. Manfred Stanley, "The Technicist Projection," Harvard University Program on Technology and Society (Fifth Annual Report, 1968-69), pp. 14-17. A theological example of technological pessimism is found in Emil Brunner, *Christianity and Civilisation* (New York: Charles Scribner's Sons, 1949), part 2. A symposium dealing with Ellul is *The Technological Order*, ed. Carl Stover (Detroit, Mich.: Wayne State University Press, 1963).
2. See Lynn White, Jr., *Medieval Technology and Social Change* (Oxford: Clarendon Press, 1962), p. 125.
3. See William Kuhns, *The Post-Industrial Prophets* (New York: Weybright and Talley, 1971), for a discussion of some of these thinkers. See especially pp. 11-115.
4. Crane Brinton, *The Shaping of the Modern Mind* (New York: New American Library [Mentor Book, paper], 1953), p. 113.
5. See Reinhold Niebuhr, *Faith and History* (New York: Charles Scribner's Sons, 1949).
6. See Carl Becker, *The Heavenly City of the Eighteenth-Century Philosophers* (New Haven, Conn.: Yale University Press, 1932).
7. R. Buckminster Fuller, *Utopia or Oblivion* (New York: Bantam Books [paper], 1969; Overlook Press, 1972).
8. See three articles in *The Futurist* by Seaborg: "Some Long-Range Implications of Nuclear Energy" (February

1968), pp. 12-13; "The New Optimism" (December 1969), pp. 157-160; and "The Birthpangs of a New World" (December 1970), pp. 205-208. See also *Man and Atom: Building a New World through Nuclear Technology* by Seaborg and William Corliss (New York: E. P. Dutton & Co., 1971).

9. See, for example, an article by Olaf Helmer of the Institute of the Future, Middletown, Conn., "New Attitudes Toward the Future," *The Futurist* (February 1967), p. 8. *The Futurist*, published by the World Future Society, is filled with confident claims of this kind, as well as more pessimistic points of view. See also Helmer et al., *Social Technology* (New York: Basic Books, Inc., 1966).
10. See B. F. Skinner's utopian novel, *Walden Two* (New York: The Macmillan Co. [paper], 1969).
11. *New York Times* (September 27, 1974), p. 41.
12. Seidenberg, *Posthistoric Man*. See also his *The Anatomy of the Future* (Chapel Hill: University of North Carolina Press, 1961).
13. Mumford, *The Pentagon of Power*, plates 14-15, between pp. 180-181.
14. W. La Barre, quoted by John McHale, *The Future of the Future* (New York: George Braziller, 1969; Ballantine Books, Inc. [paper], 1971), p. 92.
15. *Medieval Technology and Social Change*, p. 28.
16. See Lynn White, Jr., "What Accelerated Technological Progress in the Western Middle Ages?" in *Creation: The Impact of an Idea*, ed. Daniel O'Connor and Francis Oakley (New York: Charles Scribner's Sons [paper], 1969), pp. 84-104. See also White, *Machina Ex Deo* (Cambridge, Mass.: MIT Press, 1968).
17. Kenneth Boulding, "The Interplay of Technology and Values: The Emerging Superculture" in *Values and the Future*, ed. Kurt Baier and Nicholas Rescher (New York: The Free Press, 1969), p. 345.
18. See Emmanuel Mesthene, *Technological Change* (Cambridge, Mass.: Harvard University Press, 1970). Mesthene's book contains a useful discussion of many of the issues in the rest of this chapter.

19. Jerome B. Wiesner and Herbert F. York, "National Security and the Nuclear-Test Ban," *Scientific American*, 211 (October 1964), pp. 27ff.
20. Garrett Hardin, "The Tragedy of the Commons," *Science* (December 13, 1968), pp. 1243-48.
21. Harvey Brooks, *Can Science Be Planned?* Harvard University Program on Technology and Society (Reprint No. 3, 1967).
22. The claim is that of John Kenneth Galbraith, in Mesthene, *Technological Change*, p. 72.
23. Professor Weizsäcker made this point in a lecture at Kirkridge, Pennsylvania, September 1971.
24. Mumford, *Technics and Civilization* (New York: Harcourt, Brace & World [paper], 1963). Cf. Kuhns, *The Post-Industrial Prophets*, pp. 45-48.
25. In the section that follows, I am greatly indebted to a paper by Harvey Brooks, "Technology and Values," *Zygon* (March 1973), pp. 17-35.
26. "The Week in Review," *New York Times* (October 1, 1972), section 4, p. 9.
27. Brooks, "Technology and Values," pp. 34-35.

Chapter 4: Living Between Efficiency and Ecstasy

1. See Skinner's *Beyond Freedom and Dignity* (New York: Alfred A. Knopf, 1971).
2. Donella H. Meadows et al., *The Limits to Growth* (Washington, D. C.: Potomac Associates, 1972).
3. For a similar criticism of scientific reason, see my *Science, Secularization and God* (Nashville: Abingdon Press, 1969), esp. pp. 49-61, 90-115.
4. Cf. Robert Nisbet, "The Impact of Technology on Ethical Decision-Making," *The Technological Threat*, ed. Jack D. Douglas (Englewood Cliffs, N. J.: Prentice-Hall, Inc., 1971), pp. 39-54.
5. Cf. Robert Boguslaw, *The New Utopians* (Englewood Cliffs, N. J.: Prentice-Hall, Inc., 1965), pp. 34-35.
6. *The New Utopians*, p. 196.

7. *Science, Secularization and God*, pp. 49-75.
8. Alfred North Whitehead, *The Function of Reason* (Princeton, N. J.: Princeton University Press, 1929; Boston: Beacon Press [paper], 1958), p. 10.
9. *The Function of Reason*, p. 8.
10. *The Function of Reason*, p. 8.
11. Augustine, *The City of God*, trans. Marcus Dodds (New York: Random House, 1950), Book XI, Chapter 27, p. 371.
12. I have developed these ideas in previous writings. See *Science, Secularization and God*, pp. 94-109, 226-229; *Christian Biopolitics* (Nashville: Abingdon Press, 1971), pp. 108-113.
13. For a detailed interpretation of these processes in organizations, see Kenneth Boulding, *The Organizational Revolution* (New York: Harper & Brothers, 1953; Chicago: Quadrangle Books [paper], 1968), pp. xvi-xxxiv, 66-86.
14. See *The Organizational Revolution*, pp. 66-86.

Chapter 5: Living on Earth for Heaven's Sake

1. See John Bright, *The Kingdom of God* (Nashville: Abingdon-Cokesbury Press, 1953).
2. I am indebted to C. H. Dodd for this basic thesis. See his *Gospel and Law* (New York: Columbia University Press, 1951), p. 71.
3. *Gospel and Law*, pp. 3-24.
4. This thesis is explored in detail in my *Science, Secularization and God* (Nashville: Abingdon Press, 1969).
5. Toffler, *Future Shock* (New York: Random House, 1970), p. 413.
6. Cauthen, *Christian Biopolitics* (Nashville: Abingdon Press, 1971), pp. 114-116.

Chapter 6: A Declaration of Interdependence

1. Philip M. Stern, *The Great Treasury Raid* (New York: Random House, 1964).

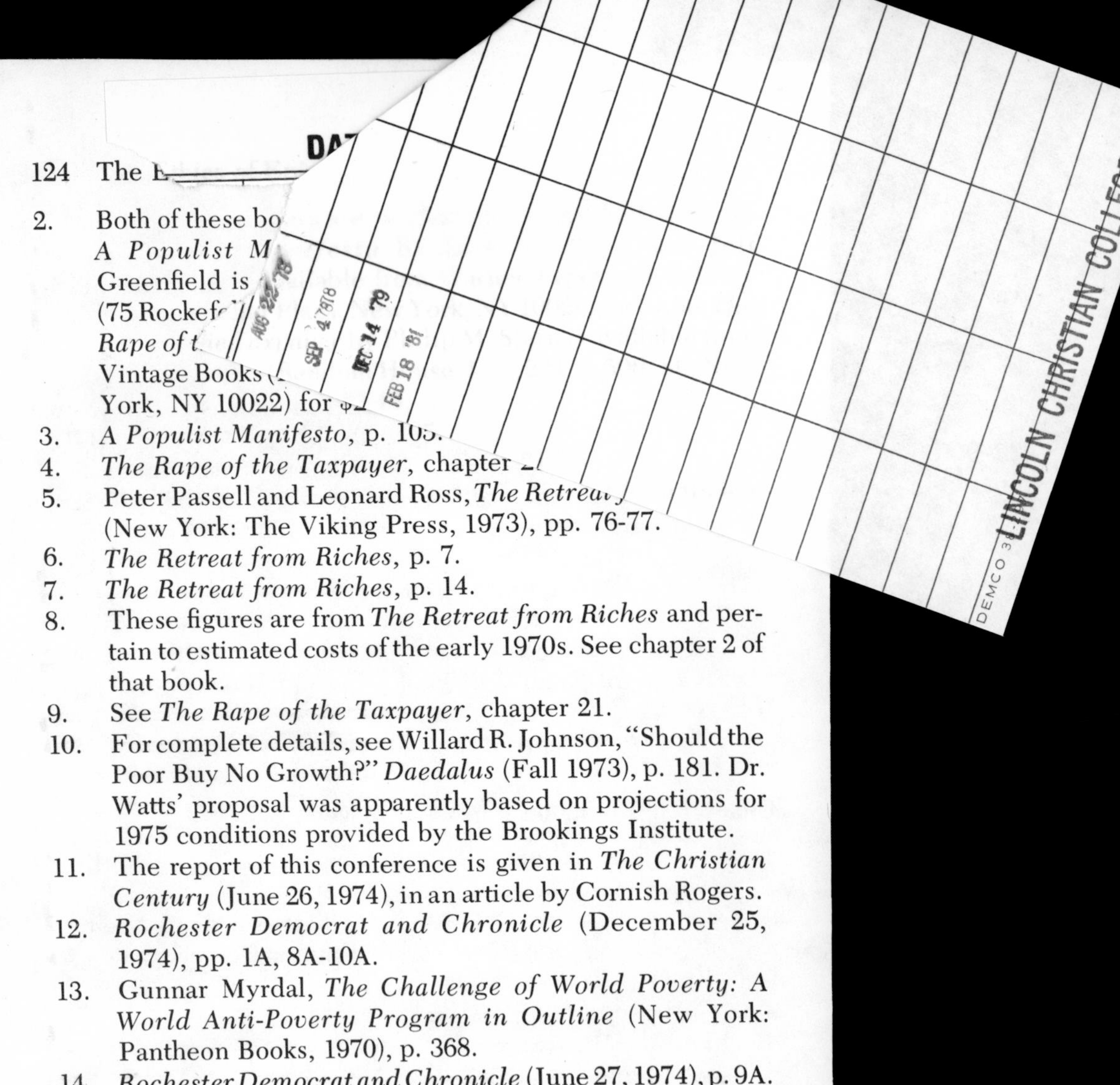

2. Both of these bo
A Populist M
Greenfield is
(75 Rockefe
Rape of t
Vintage Books (
York, NY 10022) for $
3. *A Populist Manifesto*, p. 105.
4. *The Rape of the Taxpayer*, chapter 2
5. Peter Passell and Leonard Ross, *The Retreat*
(New York: The Viking Press, 1973), pp. 76-77.
6. *The Retreat from Riches*, p. 7.
7. *The Retreat from Riches*, p. 14.
8. These figures are from *The Retreat from Riches* and pertain to estimated costs of the early 1970s. See chapter 2 of that book.
9. See *The Rape of the Taxpayer*, chapter 21.
10. For complete details, see Willard R. Johnson, "Should the Poor Buy No Growth?" *Daedalus* (Fall 1973), p. 181. Dr. Watts' proposal was apparently based on projections for 1975 conditions provided by the Brookings Institute.
11. The report of this conference is given in *The Christian Century* (June 26, 1974), in an article by Cornish Rogers.
12. *Rochester Democrat and Chronicle* (December 25, 1974), pp. 1A, 8A-10A.
13. Gunnar Myrdal, *The Challenge of World Poverty: A World Anti-Poverty Program in Outline* (New York: Pantheon Books, 1970), p. 368.
14. *Rochester Democrat and Chronicle* (June 27, 1974), p. 9A.